VENTURE DEBT DEALS

VENTURE
DEBT

DEALS

HOW TO FUND GROWTH WITH LESS DILUTION
MARSHALL HAWKS

Writing is Hard Publishing
San Francisco, California

@2026 Writing is Hard LLC
All rights reserved.
Writing is Hard Publishing is an imprint of Writing is Hard LLC.

ISBN: 978-8-9985679-0-2 (print)
ISBN: 978-8-9985679-1-9 (eBook)
ISBN: 979-8-9985679-2-6 (audiobook)

Library of Congress Control Number: 2025922074

Proofreading and Index by Heather Pendley
Design and layout by *the*BookDesigners

First edition
Printed in the United States of America
Global Distribution by Ingram Content Group

To order bulk copies of this book for use in your own programs and offerings, please contact Marshall via venturedebtdeals.com or marshallhawks.com. Thank you.

To Michelle, Cooper, and Iva

CONTENTS

INTRODUCTION. 1
Why Now? 1
Why Me?. 2
Who Is This For?. 3
How to Read This Book. 3

CHAPTER 1: THE WORLD OF VENTURE DEBT. 7
What Is Not Venture Debt? 8
Why Would You Want This Money? 8
Lenders and Their Business Models. 10
The Mechanics of Venture Debt 13
Lender Landscape. 16
Market Terms 16

CASE STUDY: *Video Game Streaming, as It Turns Out,*
Is a Great Business—Twitch. 18
Aftermath. 26
Key Takeaways. 27

CHAPTER 2: TIMELINES AND PROCESS 29
Initial Screening 29
The Diligence List. 31
Indication of Interest 34
The Term Sheet 36
After the Term Sheet 36
Final Diligence and Internal Approval 37
Legal Documentation 38

Things That Slow Down a Venture Debt Fundraise That
    Aren't Obvious. 40

CHAPTER 3: HOW BANKS AND PRIVATE CREDIT
FUNDS ARE STRUCTURED. **41**

Origination and Business Development 41
Relationship and Portfolio Management 43
Credit Officers and Investment Committee Members. 44
Special Assets, Special Loans, Advisory Services,
    or the Workout Group 47

CHAPTER 4: HOW LENDERS EVALUATE COMPANIES. **51**

Sources of Repayment 52
The Cap Table 53
Investor Diligence Calls 54
Financials and KPIs 56
Market Comps, Vertical, and Competitive Landscape 58
Team 59
Intangibles 59
This Is Art, Not Science. 60

CASE STUDY: *No (Air)Mattresses Were Harmed in the*
Making of This Film—Airbnb 61
Aftermath. 68
Key Takeaways. 69

CHAPTER 5: OVERVIEW AND STRUCTURAL
COMPONENTS OF THE TERM SHEET. **73**

Preamble. 74
Borrower(s). 75
Commitment Amount. 77
Use of Proceeds. 78

Lender(s). 78

Availability. 79

Draw Period. 80

Borrowing Formula 82

Interest-Only Period 82

Amortization Period or Repayment. 84

Maturity Date 85

Financial Covenants. 85

CHAPTER 6: ECONOMIC COMPONENTS OF THE TERM SHEET. . . 89

Interest Rate. 89

Up-Front Fees 91

Prepayment Fees. 92

Back-End Fees 95

Warrants. 96

Right to Invest. 101

Good Faith Deposit or Due Diligence Fee 102

Expenses. 103

CASE STUDY: *A Week That Will Live in Infamy—SVB* 105

Aftermath. 113

Key Takeaways. 116

CHAPTER 7: CONTROL COMPONENTS OF THE TERM SHEET. . . 119

Reporting Requirements. 120

Banking Requirements 123

Events of Default. 127

Materially Adverse Change (MAC) Clauses. 130

Investor Abandonment Clause 135

Contingency Funding Clause 137

Collateral 139

Senior and Junior Lien Positions. 143

CHAPTER 8: OTHER COMPONENTS OF THE TERM SHEET...147

Marketing... 148
Closing Conditions.................................... 149
Confidentiality 150
Exclusivity and No-Shop Clause........................ 150

CASE STUDY: *Surprises Are Only Good for Birthdays*
and Anniversaries—Phone Tap 152
Aftermath... 155
Key Takeaways... 156

CHAPTER 9: RUNNING AN EFFICIENT LEGAL PROCESS ...159

The Perfection Certificate............................ 159
Best Practices.. 162

CHAPTER 10: GET MORE FROM YOUR LENDING PARTNER...167

Share the Positive and the Negative 167
Be Proactive.. 168
Be Direct... 169
Avoid Surprises If Possible 170
Under-Promise and Over-Deliver........................ 171
Put Your Lender to Work in Unique Ways................ 172

CASE STUDY: *A Company with Nine Lives—Clearco* 177
Aftermath... 189
Key Takeaways... 190

CHAPTER 11: RED FLAGS THAT MAKE LENDERS CAUTIOUS...193

Less than 12 Months of Cash........................... 194
A Solo Lead Investor 195

The Orphaned Portfolio Company.......................... 197

There Is No Board...................................... 199

Debt Larger Than Investment from the
    Largest Shareholder 200

Debt Greater Than Revenue............................. 201

CHAPTER 12: RED FLAGS THAT SHOULD MAKE ENTREPRENEURS CAUTIOUS. 203

Personal Guarantees 203

New Entrants.. 204

Renegotiating Terms 205

Junior Team Members.................................. 206

CHAPTER 13: THE POTENTIAL DOWNSIDES OF VENTURE DEBT 209

Picking the Wrong Lending Partner 210

Not Having a Clear Use Case............................ 210

Over-Leveraging the Business........................... 212

Is It Really Worth It? 213

Author's Note... 215

Acknowledgments 217

Appendix 1: Example Term Sheet—Early-Stage 221

Appendix 2: Example Term Sheet—Later-Stage 225

Appendix 3: Marshall's Portfolio Companies
    Over the Years 231

Notes on Sources..................................... 233

Index 235

About the Author 245

INTRODUCTION

I first had the idea for this book after reading *Venture Deals* by Brad Feld and Jason Mendelson when it came out in 2011. It gave everyone in the innovation ecosystem an inside view into the venture capital fundraising process. *What is in your average VC term sheet? What do the terms mean? How do VC firms think and make decisions?* It was a great book even for those of us already immersed in the industry and is required reading for entrepreneurs to this day. If you haven't read *Venture Deals*, put this book down, go buy a copy, and read it. I'll wait.

While I loved *Venture Deals* and was inspired by it, the book only briefly discussed venture debt in the most recent edition. In this book, I want to give the topic its full due, structured in a style similar to *Venture Deals*. Why would a founder or company want to use this type of financing in the first place? How long does a debt fundraising process take? What are the common terms and their meaning? How do lenders think and make decisions? Ideally, it will help entrepreneurs, investors, lenders, and you to be more informed about venture lending from the start and save time while building better working relationships in the future.

WHY NOW?

Venture debt goes back more than forty years. The first private credit fund focused on the innovation economy, Western Technology Investment (WTI), was founded in 1980. Silicon Valley Bank (SVB), my former employer and the first bank to provide venture debt, was founded a few years later, in 1983. Venture leasing, which is equipment financing for venture-backed companies, goes even further back to the founding of Comdisco in 1969.

Even with more than forty years of history, venture debt, like venture capital and the whole of the innovation economy, was much more of a cottage industry for most of that time. Fast-forward to the present day and the tech economy is everywhere; start-up companies and investors are focused on every industry niche. The pace of innovation is affecting every business to one degree or another. And venture debt is no longer a cottage industry, with funding levels hitting an all-time high of $53B in 2024, more than four times the amount of a decade prior. Fundings in 2025 are on pace to meet and potentially ecplise that level. The pool of venture debt lenders has never been bigger and their capacity to grow with companies has never been greater. Venture debt transactions for later-stage companies are now regularly north of $100M, a scale unheard of over the last forty years. Seemed like perfect timing for a book on the topic. It also felt important to get this book published sooner rather than later, before LLMs take over all the book writing responsibilities from us mere humans.

WHY ME?

I spent over twenty years as a venture lender. The last sixteen were at SVB across three countries and nine different roles, a traumatizing bank failure, and an inspiring bank resurgence. I've had the opportunity to work with thousands of entrepreneurs, companies, and investors in that time. SVB continues to be a great firm, filled with good humans. But I felt like I needed to leave to write this book for three reasons: First, writing a book, as I've discovered, is not a small task. Balancing that while holding down a day job at SVB didn't seem conducive to my sanity or having an ongoing relationship with my family. Second, I like (some) lawyers, but if you write a book while employed at a large corporation, the amount of legal review involved before publishing is "substantial." Last, if I were to write this book while working in the industry, even at a firm like SVB, the perception of potential bias or questions about whether this was a marketing piece would have been too much.

WHO IS THIS FOR?

The primary audience for this book is tech entrepreneurs, founders, and finance folks (CFOs, VPs of Finance, etc.) who haven't yet been exposed to venture lending or have a limited understanding and want to learn more. I've done my best to make the topic approachable and assume no preexisting knowledge of venture debt or what makes lenders tick, although a basic understanding of the innovation economy and venture capital will be useful. There are a few specialized niches within the innovation ecosystem, particularly in the life science and healthcare vertical, which have a small subset of lenders who work with those companies. The topics I cover in the book are mostly focused on the tech ecosystem but will also be directionally correct for those specialized areas. However, the details of how lenders structure or approach their underwriting in those specialized industries may vary.

I've also tried to reach enough depth and nuance that seasoned entrepreneurs and finance teams will still benefit from the book's content. The same is true of my fellow lenders, investors, lawyers, and other service providers who work in and around the innovation ecosystem. I hope those groups will get value out of the more nuanced areas I've covered and, at a minimum, will now have license to give me unvarnished feedback on the book—good or bad—the next time I see them in person. Since they were nice enough to buy a copy.

HOW TO READ THIS BOOK

One way to read this book is as a reference guide. If you're an entrepreneur, founder, or CFO amid an active venture debt discussion with lenders, you may want to jump to Chapters 5 through 8, which provide a deep dive into the different components of a term sheet. Those chapters will help you compare what you are seeing in proposals from lenders versus what I cover in the book. If you are already working with a lender in the innovation space, I'd suggest jumping to Chapter 10 to make sure you are getting everything you can out of that relationship. If you enjoy good stories, there are five case studies involving my former portfolio companies and my former employer sprinkled throughout the book. Perhaps starting there would be a good choice. Regardless, you have my permission to jump around the book as needed. If you are completely new to this topic or just a traditionalist, reading the book from front to back should set you up nicely.

The topic of venture debt, like any financial topic, can be complex and takes time to fully understand. Like any financial instrument, it has its own "language," acronyms, misconceptions, jargon, and nomenclature—as well as market norms that venture lenders know and adhere to. I've structured the book chronologically based on when a particular topic comes up during a normal venture debt process:

The World of Venture Debt: Chapter 1

What is venture debt and why would any company consider using it? What are the mechanics of an average deal? Who are the major providers of venture debt in the innovation economy? What are normal market terms you can expect to see from most lenders?

Process, Timing, and Thought Process: Chapters 2–4

What does a venture debt process look like from start to finish? What will be on most lenders' diligence lists, how many meetings will they want, and who on your team will they want to meet? How much time will you need to devote to this process to do it right? How are these firms structured, what are the various roles within each firm, and how do they make decisions?

The Term Sheet: Chapters 5–8

In this section, we break down a venture debt term sheet and provide a full overview of the various components. What does each section or term mean? How might these terms vary based on the stage of the company (early, mid, or later)? What are lenders thinking about in the background? Last, what are key considerations for founders during the give-and-take of negotiations? This is the most complex part of the book but also, ideally, the most useful.

All Things Legal—Chapter 9

I heart lawyers. So much so that I basically gave them their own section in the book. Two great firms, Fenwick & West (they represent companies) and DLA Piper LLP (US-they represent lenders), cover a variety of best practices for how to run an efficient legal process.

The Stuff That Really Matters: Chapters 10–12

Term sheets and legal documents are important, but at the end of the day, the success of lending relationships really comes down to the humans involved. This part of the book covers how to build a solid working relationship between company and lender, plus some common pitfalls between those parties that I've seen over the past two decades.

The Downsides of Venture Debt—Chapter 13

Any good debate team member would tell you that while important to know your side of an issue cold, it is even more important to understand the other side's arguments, and ideally, better than they do. In this final chapter, I take the other side of the argument and cover a variety of reasons why venture debt can be bad for a company, and hopefully how to avoid getting in that situation.

Appendices and Index

Sample term sheets for both an earlier-stage company and a later-stage company are included for your reading enjoyment. I've done my best to define industry terms within the book, so I skipped a glossary for this edition. The index acts like a bit of a glossary and will also help you jump around to various sections as needed.

1

THE WORLD OF VENTURE DEBT

The simple definition of venture debt is a loan that lasts three to five years, has minimal controls or financial covenants, and extends the runway of the company using it. The reason it is called venture debt is that it sits somewhere between normal commercial lending on one side and venture capital investing on the other. It is debt that needs to be repaid, and lenders sit at the top of the repayment waterfall. But the "venture" part of venture debt is in the name because the typical company using it has little history, is almost always losing money, and may never get to cash flow-positive operations. Let's unpack this all a bit further.

Commercial lending has been around for a *long* time, going back to at least the Medicis in Florence, Italy, during the fourteenth century. The way commercial lenders evaluate which businesses they think are creditworthy and those that are not has remained consistent since that time. *Does the business have a meaningful track record? Have they consistently been able to grow? Are they profitable? Do they have assets that could serve as collateral? Is the business predictable? Can I get the owner of the business to guarantee the debt? Do I trust these people?* If you went into a training program to be a lender at any number of large banks in the world today, you would be told to ask most, if not all, of those questions of potential borrowers.

With venture debt you can take a lot of those questions and . . . throw them out the window. The typical company that uses venture debt does not have a meaningful track record. They may not have launched their product yet. They likely aren't profitable, may not have predictable revenues, and have few assets. They are the antithesis of what is considered a decent candidate for normal commercial lending. Even in good times, the default outcome for the average start-up is still failure. You might rightfully ask, *What motivates anyone to want to lend to high-risk companies in the first place?* Hold that thought.

WHAT IS NOT VENTURE DEBT?

Venture debt is not the only type of commercial lending available to venture-backed start-ups, particularly those that have started to scale. Lots of banks provide lines of credit that are revolving, similar to a credit card. Those lines of credit tend to be governed by some form of borrowing formula, like a percentage of the company's accounts receivable, for example. Or you might have a credit line tied to your recurring revenue where you can commonly borrow 3x or more of your monthly recurring revenue. Beyond lines of credit, there are many other types of lending available to companies, including acquisition financing, equipment financing, and cash flow-based structures.

As companies scale, they will gain access to this broader landscape of options from a larger chunk of commercial lenders and private credit. The options all have valid use cases and, in fact, become more prevalent than venture debt over a company's life cycle. For the purposes of this book, however, we are going to focus solely on venture debt at the expense of those other forms of financing, even if they are being offered to the same company at the same time. The primary distinction is that those other financing options typically have meaningful financial covenants and restrictions that prevent, with rare exceptions, the borrower from using the funding provided to extend runway. The "venture" part of venture debt.

WHY WOULD YOU WANT THIS MONEY?

For an entrepreneur, venture debt—like venture capital—is a tool to help capitalize their business and fund growth. Usually, venture debt provides a start-up with an extra six, nine, or twelve months of runway on top of a recent equity raise. Ideally, during the extra time or runway that the debt has provided, the company achieves an important milestone or two, adds a key customer(s) or a new critical hire, perhaps even gets to cash flow break-even. That progress, in the best case, allows the company to successfully raise a new equity round from an outside investor at a meaningfully increased valuation relative to if they had to fundraise earlier. This helps minimize dilution to the founders, employees, and existing shareholders, so that they own more of the business when there is a good outcome down the road (IPO or M&A). For more scaled businesses, venture debt can potentially be used to displace the need for a later-stage equity round ahead of getting to profitability, M&A, or IPO.

The financial impact of using less dilutive venture debt for the owners of the business can be significant. The comparatively fast process to raise venture debt versus an equity fundraise is also meaningful. Both attributes combined are what makes venture debt attractive to entrepreneurs and the companies they lead. Does every situation where venture debt is used end up like I've outlined above? Nope. Are there potential downsides to using venture debt? Yep. We will cover a number of those possibilities in Chapter 13. Just like venture capital, there are pros and cons to using venture debt to capitalize your business. Knowing when and how to use it appropriately has the potential to keep your business alive and/or help to keep more of the upside in your pocket down the road.

The following is a nice visualization of the potential impact of venture debt over time:

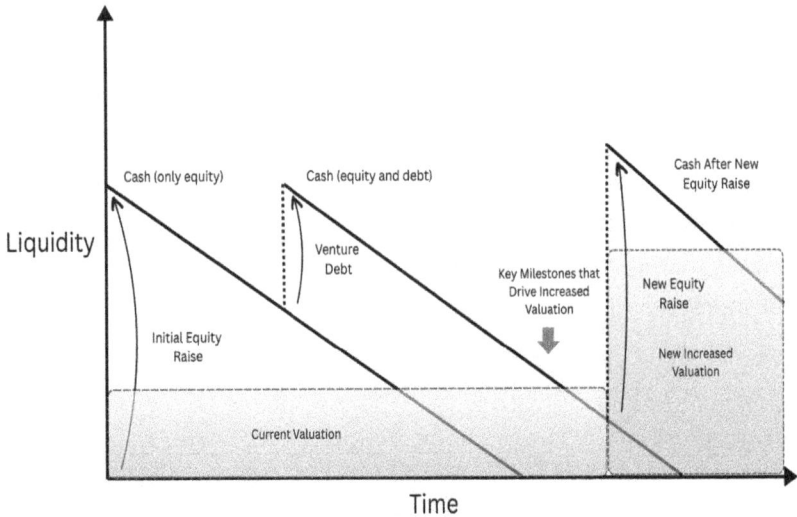

Cash (only equity)

Cash (equity and debt)

Cash After New Equity Raise

Liquidity

Venture Debt

Key Milestones that Drive Increased Valuation

New Equity Raise

Initial Equity Raise

New Increased Valuation

Current Valuation

Time

LENDERS AND THEIR BUSINESS MODELS

In the innovation economy, there are two primary types of lenders, and they each have different funding sources, business models, and processes.

The first type of venture debt lender is commercial banks. Out of the thousands of banks in the US, only a small subset focuses on VC-backed companies and the innovation ecosystem. Those banks use the deposits of customers with excess cash as the primary source of funding for their venture debt loans. They then lend that cash to other customers who need to borrow money. Essentially, Banking 101: You take money from companies that have it and lend it to companies that need it. If a bank doesn't have enough creditworthy companies that want to borrow, they will take those excess deposits and invest them, ideally in things that won't cause the bank to fail (inside joke about SVB's failure, one of a few throughout this book—thanks for bearing with my banking humor). What does it matter where the money to provide venture debt comes from? The cost of capital. Banks have an inexpensive source of funds (excess deposits), which means venture debt from banks will generally be less expensive.

Banks are regulated by one or more governmental entities (FDIC, OCC, state regulators, etc.) based on the size, complexity, and geographic footprint of the institution.

The other primary type of venture debt lender is private credit funds ("private credit"). Private credit is a broad term that encompasses several types of funds that raise money differently but also collectively differ from commercial banks. Private credit funds don't take customer deposits because they are not banks. They raise money from third-party investors or limited partners who expect their capital back plus a good return in the future. This means that debt from private credit funds tends to be more expensive when compared to bank lenders but oftentimes is larger and more flexible.

Some private credit funds, as the name would suggest, are fully private entities, but some are publicly traded. Although the private credit world is significantly less regulated than banks, it does have some oversight from the SEC or other governmental bodies depending on how the firm is structured. In the US, banks and private credit funds are the two main parties that lend to venture-backed start-ups. In international markets, you may find a more prominent third type of lender, government-backed funds. In Canada, for example, several players are active in the venture-backed ecosystem. Business Development Bank of Canada and Export Development Canada are two good examples. For the purposes of this book, at least in the first edition, the focus is solely on banks and non-governmental private credit funds. Sadly, government players will have to wait.

Commercial banks that provide venture debt are mostly lending to earlier-stage companies, such as start-ups that have raised their Series A or B round of equity financing and are looking for less than $20M in venture debt. Banks want to work with companies early in their life cycle because they are playing a portfolio theory and lifetime value game. They use venture debt largely as a customer acquisition tool. Lend a start-up some money early on, get all their banking business (a requirement of this type of lending, with some nuance post-SVB's failure), and if they do a good job building a relationship, they get the benefit of working with that company for years. Banks aren't really making a bet that any individual portfolio company will become the next Apple or SpaceX. If they were great at that, they would become investors and make a lot more money. They are playing the odds that, on average, a company that has raised a Series A will go on to raise a Series B from new investors or from their existing shareholders. That new equity will then help pay down or pay off the outstanding venture debt, the ultimate outcome of the business notwithstanding.

Banks are generally more focused than private credit firms on the venture investors during their underwriting since most earlier-stage companies will not have significant financial metrics to evaluate. Has the bank worked with the venture fund(s) or partner before? Is the fund newly raised or several years old? What is the history of the firm follow-on investing into their portfolio companies? Any good or bad experience working through downside situations? These are some of the questions bank lenders will be thinking about early on. Banks are hoping to build out a portfolio of borrowers that is granular, both to mitigate risk and to increase the chance of working with a few breakout companies that will have significant lifetime value. If you asked most of the bank lenders out there, they would say they are trying to lend a start-up as little money as possible while still winning the company's business.

In contrast, most private credit funds focus primarily on later-stage start-ups—companies that typically are looking for $30M or more of venture debt. A few private credit funds also focus on very early, seed-stage companies, hoping to gain equity investment rights in the process. All private credit funds are the same in that they are not trying to acquire a customer to get deposits; in fact, they don't care about deposits at all. One of the selling points of private credit funds is that you, as a company, can keep your banking relationship wherever you want. Private credit funds are more often looking to find the better companies in a particular space, i.e., trying to pick winners, and consequently spend more time looking at the performance of the business, customer data, metrics, etc. Scaled businesses have more to evaluate and you can even start to compare them to similar public company profiles. Private credit funds evaluate investor syndicates too, asking a lot of the same questions that banks ask, but it is not their only significant area of diligence.

All things being equal, taking a venture debt loan from a private credit fund tends to be more transactional. They don't get the benefit of a broader banking relationship, and once the need for the debt goes away, that firm fades out of the picture. So, they are understandably focused on generating a return for the dollars they lend. This does not mean all private credit funds are purely transactional in the negative sense. The best private credit funds build long-lasting relationships with entrepreneurs and investors in the hopes of providing larger loans as the company grows or the opportunity to fund multiple portfolio companies within a particular venture firm over time.

Do private credit funds work with earlier-stage companies? Occasionally. Do banks sometimes provide larger chunks of venture debt to scaled businesses? Occasionally. Is there a big gray area in the middle between early- and later-stage companies where both types of lenders are active? Definitely.

THE MECHANICS OF VENTURE DEBT

Let's expand on the simple definition I provided. Venture debt is most often on the heels of a venture capital financing. Lenders like to come in at that point because not only does the company in question have eighteen to thirty-six months of runway from its own equity dollars, but it also has fresh validation from outside investors who have done their own diligence on the business. Insert your favorite joke on the caliber of VC diligence here . . .

For early-stage companies (Series A or B), the amount of venture debt lenders are willing to provide, assuming they are comfortable with the business in the first place, tends to be a percentage of the dollars raised in the most recent equity round. Normally that would range between 25% and 40% of the latest equity round. If an equity round gets outsized, say $50M or more, then the percentage lenders are comfortable to provide drops to the low end of the range, and perhaps even smaller. As a company scales and begins to have meaningful revenue, the amount of venture debt available to the business shifts to a percentage or even a multiple of revenue. A good rule of thumb would be 0.5× to 1× trailing twelve months revenue or the more forward-looking ARR (annual recurring revenue).

Regardless of the size of the venture debt, the company will have some time frame to use or draw down the money (called the drawdown period). A drawdown period today may range from six to twenty-four months, depending on the situation and firm providing the debt capital. Running concurrently with the drawdown period is the interest-only period. If the company has borrowed any amount of the venture debt, this is where they only have to make monthly interest payments; no principal payments or amortization are required. An average interest-only period is eighteen to twenty-four months, at which point the amortization period kicks in. This is when the business starts to pay principal and interest, typically in equal monthly payments, over an average of three years. So, the total time frame of the debt I've just described looks something like this:

Loan is closed and funds are now available	Draw Period & Interest-Only Period	Amortization Period		Loan is fully paid off
	18–24 Months	36 Months		
	5 Year Total Duration			
Time ———>				

When taking debt from private credit, draw periods tend to be shorter because funds want to start earning a return, but the interest-only periods tend to be longer, potentially ranging from three to six years. There may be an amortization period, but it is also possible that the outstanding debt is all repaid at the end. So, the total time frame would then look something like this:

	Draw Period			
Loan is closed and funds are now available	0–6 Months			Loan is fully paid off
	Interest-Only Period			
	36–60 Months			
	5 Year Total Duration			
	Time ———>			

In many venture debt transactions, particularly for earlier-stage companies, there won't be any financial covenants or milestones restricting how a company can access the money or any kind of borrowing formula tied to assets or revenue. Once the company has borrowed the money, there also won't likely be any ongoing financial performance measurement or covenants. In normal commercial lending to non-venture-backed businesses, and for later-stage venture debt transactions, it is more common to see financial covenants. Those covenants measure things like revenue to plan, minimum cash or liquidity levels, and holding debt to revenue under a certain multiple.

The cost of this type of financing is a combination of fees, interest rate on the borrowed dollars, and a warrant for a small amount of ownership in your company. Don't worry, we cover all of this in much more detail in Chapters 5 through 8.

LENDER LANDSCAPE

This is my non-exhaustive list of the active venture lenders in North America as of the beginning of 2026. *Active* is defined as a firm currently bidding on new business, regardless of total deals done. Banks generally will be more active in the market given that they tend to bid on earlier-stage opportunities, which are more numerous. Private credit funds will individually and collectively work with fewer total companies, but the average dollar size of their deals will be significantly larger than for banks. Are there lenders not captured here who provide venture debt? Very likely. But I'd guess this list covers 90% of venture debt transactions done in North America over the past two to three years.

MARKET TERMS

We will walk through, in detail, the process of putting venture debt in place in Chapters 2 through 4, and the components of a venture debt term sheet in Chapters 5 through 8 of this book. However, I didn't want you to have to wait until then to get a quick snapshot of the market—both the lenders and the current market terms from those players (see below). I've bucketed the market into four stages. Seed, early-stage, mid-stage, and later-stage. These are generalized terms for a company at each stage that will obviously vary for any individual situation. There can be a lot of gray area between these buckets, depending on the individual company profile, so don't take this as gospel.

Stage of Company	Seed	Early Stage	Mid Stage	Later Stage
Size of Debt	<$3.5M	Up to $15M	$15M-$35M	$35M+
Lenders	A few funds and 1-2 banks	All banks and occasionally funds	Most banks and most funds	All funds and occasionally banks
Covenants	No	Occasionally	Likely	Yes
Milestones	Possible	Possible	Possible	Possible
Interest Rate	WSJ Prime + 1.0%-2.5%	WSJ Prime + 0.5%-1.5%	WSJ Prime + 0.5%-1.5%	WSJ Prime + 3.0%-6.0%
Fees	0.25%-0.50%	0%-0.25%	0.25%-0.50%	0.50%-1.25%
Warrants (FDO)	25-75bps	10-30bps	10-30bps	15-75bps

Banks

- Avidbank
- Banc of California (fka PacWest)
- Bridge Bank
- CIBC (Canada & US)
- Comerica Bank
- East West Bank
- HSBC Innovation Banking
- JP Morgan Disruptive Commerce
- LIve Oak Bank
- National Bank (Canada)
- RBCx (Canada)
- Stifel Venture Bank
- SVB, a Division of First Citizens Bank
- TD Innovation Partners (Canada)

Private Credit

- Alliance Bernstein
- Apollo
- Ares
- ATEL Ventures
- Blackrock
- BDC Capital (Canada)
- Columbia Lake Partners
- Costella Kirsch
- Escalate Capital Partners
- Espresso Capital
- Flow Capital
- Fortress
- Golub
- Hercules
- Horizon Technology Finance

Private Credit (cont'd)

- InnoVen Capital
- Kreos (Europe)
- LAGO Innovation Fund
- Lighter Capital
- Lighthouse
- Liquidity Group
- MidCap
- Montage Capital
- Multiplier Capital
- Neuberger Berman
- Oaktree
- Orix
- ORIX Growth Capital
- Overlap Holdings
- Owl Rock
- Oxford
- Partners for Growth
- PIMCO
- Pinegrove Credit
- Runway Growth Capital
- Silver Lake Waterman
- Sixth Street
- SQN Venture Partners
- Structural Capital
- Symbiotic Capital
- Tacora Capital
- Top Corner Capital
- TPG
- Trinity
- TriplePoint Ventures
- Vistara Growth
- WTI (aka Venture Lending & Leasing)

CASE STUDY

VIDEO GAME STREAMING, AS IT TURNS OUT, IS A GREAT BUSINESS—TWITCH

The four primary case studies you'll find in the book were selected because (1) they give you a sense of how venture debt is used in the real world, (2) they grapple with issues discussed throughout the book, (3) they span a range of outcomes, (4) I was the lender to each company, and (5) they are interesting stories in their own right. The fifth case study is a bit different; it's about SVB and the impact the bank's failure had on the venture debt landscape.

Among the video game playing crowd and younger people in general, Twitch is a household name. It continues to be the leader in the video game streaming world after creating the category in the first place, allowing pro players and amateurs alike to broadcast their digital exploits for the world to see. Twitch was acquired by Amazon in 2014 for a little over a $1B in cash and continues to be an independent division within the broader company. In 2024, Twitch had over 240M monthly active users, 21 billion hours of content were consumed, and the average user spent north of ninety minutes per day on the site—close to double the time users spent on TikTok, Twitter/X, or Instagram. But before becoming one of the top five broadband consumers on the whole of the internet, Twitch had more humble beginnings.

Justin.tv was founded in 2006 by Justin Kan, Emmett Shear, Michael Seibel, and Kyle Vogt as a general-purpose live streaming video platform. In classic Silicon Valley fashion, they hadn't quite figured out the business model but knew that if they were attracting users, they could worry about that later. How did they attract their initial users? By having co-founder Justin Kan (namesake of

Justin.tv) strap a camera to his head and live stream his life 24/7, of course. In today's hyper-online environment, this kind of stunt would be met with a yawn, but in 2007, this was must-see (online) TV for the tech world. The company went through Y Combinator's winter 2007 batch and then raised a Series A investment led by Alsop Louie Partners shortly thereafter.

I joined SVB in January 2009 as a relationship manager (RM) on the only lending team the bank had based in San Francisco and when the broader financial and banking world was melting down. At the time, most people in the innovation economy didn't think much about San Francisco. In fact, SVB had a hard time finding people who wanted to live and work in the city. How times have changed since then. As a newly minted RM at any bank, you are typically given an existing portfolio of companies to manage. In my case, the handful of companies included a small venture debt deal in legal documents to a company called Justin.tv. I helped to close that initial transaction in 2009 and would end up putting in place another four debt facilities totaling $20M before the company's eventual acquisition by Amazon five years down the road.

Why did Justin.tv need to borrow so much money? Well, in 2009, cloud computing was still in its nascent stage and building a platform that hosted live streaming video was very bandwidth intensive. So, in addition to normal start-up operating expenses like headcount and rent, Justin.tv was burning through capital building out their own server infrastructure that was all on-premises while trying to figure out the early innings of an advertising-based business model. Advertising is a tough business model because it can be unpredictable. The rate that marketers will pay to place an ad on your site fluctuates regularly. Further, that revenue is also dependent on having enough users in the right demographic around to look at those ads. Said another way, Justin.tv's first few years of existence had a lot of ups and downs, which included my blood pressure as their lender. In fact, the internal credit officer at SVB at the time (the guy actually approving the debt I wanted to provide), a very senior and well-respected person, said emphatically to me in 2010, "This is the worst company in your portfolio and I'm certain they are going to fail; it's just a question of when." Since he thought we could potentially lose money on the transaction, I give him full credit for still being willing to move forward. But he was putting a stake in the ground, and for the first few years, he certainly looked to be right because Justin.tv hadn't yet figured out a sustainable business model. Even with the internal consternation about whether Justin.tv had future potential, we closed and funded our first $2.5M chunk of venture debt in Q1 2009.

The release of the original iPhone in 2007 was the moment that *mobile* became a legitimate platform. I occasionally go back to watch the original iPhone launch on YouTube. Talk about a master class by Steve Jobs in building anticipation to a fever pitch and then delivering! Worth a look if you've never seen it. Steve Jobs was an amazing presenter. But I digress.

The initial landgrab to build software and native apps for the iPhone was fierce but tempered by the lack of high-speed connectivity. It really kicked into high gear when Apple launched the iPhone 3G in June 2008 and the iPhone 3GS in June 2009. The fourth-generation iPhone had better connectivity plus a better camera that could take pictures AND video. Laughable given today's mobile technology, but this enabled a whole new set of use cases. Instagram launched the following year in October 2010 and became an immediate must-have for mobile photos. The Justin.tv team saw the same trends and launched Socialcam in March 2011. The app enabled users to quickly capture and share videos directly from their phone. Usage took off with more than 1M app downloads in the first four months and it continued ramping up from there. Justin.tv decided to spin out Socialcam into a stand-alone independent company, so each team could focus on their different priorities.

When a company takes on venture debt, it commits to get the lender's approval or buyoff for meaningful corporate decisions from that point forward. In this case, spinning out the fastest growing part of Justin.tv into a stand-alone business was a meaningful corporate decision. Effectively, we were being asked to let a portion of the business (i.e., our collateral)—that could help repay our debt—walk out the door.

SVB has always tried to be founder- and company-friendly given the innovation economy is its sole target market. The general stance of the bank, now a part of First Citizens, continues to be, how they can get to "yes." With that as backdrop, I had several conversations with Michael Siebel (CEO) about Socialcam becoming a stand-alone company and we ultimately agreed to allow the spinout. We did this in part because I wanted to be accommodating to a company and set of founders that I liked, but also because Michael and I were having a live conversation about providing a small chunk of new venture debt to Socialcam as well. That discussion was ongoing as Socialcam went back to Y Combinator in their winter 2012 class. The term sheet for that new venture debt deal was signed in early 2012 and I was working on the legal agreement with Michael and their outside counsel.

Then the news that Autodesk was acquiring Socialcam for $60M dropped in late spring of 2012. What should have been exciting news made my stomach drop because our new deal had not closed yet. We wouldn't have a warrant in Socialcam and would miss out on the now very real upside.

I was frustrated at myself and my team for not moving faster to close the new Socialcam deal. And I was very selfishly frustrated that I missed out on the direct economic upside, which would have been the biggest of my venture-lending career to date (more on individual lenders being directly compensated by warrants in Chapter 6). So, I made the fateful decision late one evening to call Michael on the heels of the acquisition announcement. I've captured the details of that call below in a segment my wife would be all too familiar with:

MARSHALL DOES SOMETHING STUPID

I got Michael on the phone and he was understandably stoked that his four-person, newly spun-out company that had raised very little equity was now being acquired. Life-changing outcome at the time for them. The tone promptly changed when I told him I was frustrated that we hadn't closed our deal, had allowed Socialcam to spin out without additional economics, and that we wanted to be compensated by being granted a warrant in the company anyway, effectively through the goodness of his heart. Michael was kind enough not to laugh at me or blow up at me over the phone. If I recall correctly, he said he would think about it and quickly hung up. I immediately realized I'd let my frustration and, frankly, greed cloud my judgment. The fact that we failed to close the new deal with Socialcam was not Michael's fault. Michael and the Justin.tv board were not to blame for the fact that we didn't ask for compensation when approving the spinout of Socialcam. I was the one at fault for not asking for additional economics when the spinout happened. And I compounded the problem by trying to walk back that decision. Something I regret to this day.

Why am I self-flagellating in front of you? Well, everybody thinks they will do the right thing in the heat of the moment. And for some people, that is true. In my case, I had to learn the hard way that it was far better to do what I said I was going to do, even if it was to my detriment, then to try and re-trade terms or attempt to change an agreement after the fact. The long-term benefit of the relationships was worth far more than optimizing for any individual outcome. Thankfully, Michael and

I got together a few years after this happened, and he was gracious enough to accept my apology for how I had acted. Solid guy.

While I was making a mockery of being a good partner with Socialcam, life carried on at Justin.tv. They had begun to monetize their sizable audience with advertising, growing annual revenues to north of $10M. But growth had started to plateau. They also continued to burn capital under the weight of high bandwidth and server costs. As Socialcam was taking off and spinning out, the Justin.tv team, now led by new CEO Emmett Shear, looked at where usage and engagement were the highest across the site. Interestingly, the slice of their audience that spent the most time on site was, of all things, people watching others play video games. Those engagement levels, the amount of time a user would spend on-site, were through the roof. People would show up and spend eighty minutes per day or more, on average, watching somebody else play a video game. This type of usage was head and shoulders above other social media or online platforms, even today. So, they made the fateful decision to pivot the company, rebrand as Twitch, and go all-in on video game streaming. They built integrations into PC games that allowed users to stream their gameplay. They were also able to strike deals with Sony and Microsoft to allow console-level integration into the PlayStation and Xbox; that meant that anyone playing a game on either console could broadcast their gameplay at the touch of a button. They built relationships across the industry and became a household name for the videogame demographic.

During this time, SVB provided Twitch with additional debt capital in rapid succession to help finance the back-end infrastructure needed to handle their growth and to help generally extend the runway. We closed new debt transactions in Q2 2012, Q1 2013, and Q4 2013. They also raised additional equity as well, closing a $15M Series B, led by Ethan Kurzweil at Bessemer, in September 2012 and a $20M Series C, led by Chris Paik at Thrive Capital, in September 2013. The company exited 2013 with 45M+ unique visitors per month—more than double the year prior, with average time on site per user increasing to more than 100 minutes per day. Explosive. Growth. Top-line revenue grew to more than $50M, still mostly on the strength of their advertising business, and the company's cash burn continued to be meaningful. The growth in usage on the site was hard to ignore, and Twitch had become the ONLY place that video game streamers and watchers wanted to be. Other big tech players had begun to take notice and expressed interest in potentially acquiring the business. The Twitch team and their board engaged Qatalyst Partners, of Frank Quattrone fame, to help navigate that inbound interest.

The initial company to show real interest in acquiring Twitch was Google. In a lot of ways, it made a ton of sense, given how Google's own business was driven by advertising and they were the de facto standard for video on demand from their ownership of YouTube. Now they could own both video on demand and live streaming. The purchase price was north of $1B, a great outcome and the largest potential acquisition I'd be involved with to date. One small problem, the company was also running out of cash. Given Twitch's impressive growth, the company would have likely had no issue raising additional equity if needed. But knowing they were in live acquisition talks that could lead to a near-term outcome meant it was a tough time to bring on new capital. Raising any equity, from outsiders or insiders, would impact the cap table, something nobody, particularly the founders and employees, wanted to see happen.

Twitch asked SVB to help bridge to the sale of the business in a way that didn't affect the cap table. We believed in the business and the people. We also believed they would be able to pivot and raise equity if the M&A discussions fell apart. Conveniently, we already had a sizable ownership stake in the business (north of 1% fully diluted), given all our prior lending to the company. We agreed to provide $10M in bridge financing, the economics of which only required a back-end fee instead of a new warrant, and Twitch would be required to close the acquisition by Google or raise equity within a set time frame.

Murphy's Law. While I don't know the full sequence of events since I wasn't in the live board discussions, shortly after providing bridge financing to the company, Google backed out of the acquisition, primarily driven by concerns over how the government would view their "monopoly" on all things online video. Seeing an acquisition of this scale fall through is never fun for anybody, but the good news was that another suitor had just come to the table. Yahoo. This was the Marissa Mayer iteration of Yahoo. She had already made a big splash in 2013 with the acquisition of Tumblr and now wanted to move Yahoo in another new direction by acquiring Twitch. The purchase price in this case was even higher: $1.5B. Legal agreements were circulated. Lots of money spent on lawyers. One of the final items that Marissa and Yahoo needed to move forward was for their own board to approve the acquisition. Most of the time, these approvals are a foregone conclusion, having been meaningfully discussed already. But in the case of Yahoo, in a surprise turn, their board decided they didn't want Yahoo acquiring Twitch. Or at least that was the story shared with the company and me/SVB. This, in hindsight, seems to be one of the early indications that Marissa Mayer's time leading Yahoo might be coming to an end.

Another few months went by and we were in the middle of 2014. Having two sizable acquisitions fall through in quick succession is a surefire way to distract any executive team. I'm sure that was true with the Twitch team, but to their credit, the business continued to grow while all this was going on. Revenues, users, and average time on site all hit new highs in 2014. And further good news—there was yet another potential acquirer who was interested in the business. Amazon.

Not the most obvious acquirer at the time, but they had a track record of allowing some of their larger acquisitions to run as independent divisions (Zappos, Audible/Goodreads, etc.), which I think appealed to the Twitch team. They were also willing to write a sizable check to bring the business in house: $970M up front in cash with meaningful retention for employees to stay on afterward. As they say, the third time's the charm. In what was its second largest acquisition to date at the time, Amazon completed its purchase of Twitch in August of 2014. The outstanding SVB debt, including the bridge loan, was fully repaid at close with the bank also making ~$20M in upside from its ownership position in the company. The upside equated to roughly the same amount of money we had put out the door to Twitch since inception. Not a bad day's work.

AFTERMATH

Post-acquisition, Twitch has continued as an independent division at Amazon as this book goes to print. It is the de facto standard for video game streaming, even with YouTube's impressive efforts. A lot of the original team, including Emmett Shear, stayed on for years within Amazon. Whether that was a joyride or a drag, you'll have to ask them directly.

I had a chance to sit down with Twitch's long-running COO and all-around nice guy, Kevin Lin, about a year after the acquisition closed. I asked whether he and the other leaders at Twitch had ever figured out what sparked Amazon's interest in buying the company. He said that they hadn't directly asked the question of Amazon leadership, but Kevin thought he knew at least part of the answer. The demographics of the core user base at Twitch were mostly young males. At the time, that group was one of the least likely subscribers to Amazon Prime. And wouldn't you know it, several years post-acquisition, Amazon's single largest source of new Prime subscribers came from the Twitch user base.

KEY TAKEAWAYS

Working with Twitch for five-plus years is one of the best examples I have of the potential benefits of using venture debt alongside equity. Obviously, the business success was driven by the founders and team at Twitch, full stop. But the venture debt we put in place allowed the company to get further with less equity capital raised. When the acquisition closed, based on our modeling at SVB, the venture debt allowed the founders and employees to avoid another 7%–10% dilution in their ownership if they had raised additional equity rounds that were contemplated. With a $1B outcome, retaining larger ownership levels meant meaningful dollars stayed in the pocket of the founders, employees, and the existing shareholders.

I learned the hard lesson that you never go back on a deal, in my case, with the spinout of Socialcam. Your ability to operate in the innovation economy is driven by your reputation, particularly if you want to spend your career in this world. Doing what you say you are going to do, every time, even if it might be to your detriment, is the price of admission. With Socialcam, we missed out on $500K of upside, due to my miss, but at the end of the day, it turned into a rounding error when compared to the upside from the acquisition of Twitch. I became a much better lender and human since learning that lesson.

Twitch is a great example of the potential network effects in Silicon Valley. The bulk of the founding and senior team went on to do more extraordinary things. Michael Seibel ran Y Combinator for years and is still there as a partner. Emmett Shear ran Twitch within Amazon for nine years post-acquisition, became the CEO at OpenAI for a hot minute, and recently started a new company. Kyle Vogt, the engineering head of Twitch, cofounded Cruise Automation. And this list goes on. Not every company will end up like Twitch, obviously, but this is what helps reinforce good behavior in the industry. Which leads to . . .

Coupled with intellectual curiosity, a good lender (or investor) in the innovation economy really needs to be willing to suspend disbelief. Willingness to talk to and help anybody, even if they are super young or even if their idea seems crazy, is a key component of what makes Silicon Valley great. You never know, they might be right.

Winning together is addictive. Twitch turned into a giant business and great financial outcome, but it was eight years after their launch and they ended up building something very different than the original idea. I had the opportunity to work with Twitch in my late twenties; it was hugely impactful for my life and made it even more gratifying to experience a situation where everyone got to win together. The founders and team at Twitch built an amazing business that is still the leader in the space to this day. The investors were communicative, humble (at least for investors), and willing to help as needed. I enjoyed spending time with and learning from the Twitch team and their board members. We at SVB were able to play a small but important part in helping capitalize the business until the acquisition. When they were acquired, we all owned a piece of the business and celebrated together. Sharing in a good outcome is one of those things that, as it turns out, is pretty unique to the innovation economy. If only they were all like this.

2

TIMELINES AND PROCESS

Compared to a venture capital fundraise, a venture debt process is shorter and requires less depth. A fast, well-run venture debt fundraise, with no unforeseen hiccups, can take as little as ninety days from initial conversation to a signed legal agreement and money available to the borrower. Can it go faster? Yes, if a borrower has a time constraint, like trying to close a big M&A transaction that involves funding debt at close, for example, and assuming all parties are equally motivated. Can it go significantly slower? For sure. The average venture debt fundraise will take four to five months to complete. Many factors can drag out the process, which we will also cover at the end of this chapter. In total, a fundraise will look something like this:

Initial Screening	Due Diligence	Term Sheet & Negotiations	Final Approval & Diligence		Total Time
			2-4 Weeks		
1-2 Days	2-4 Weeks	1-3 Weeks	Legal Documents		4-5 Months
			6-8 Weeks		
Time ———>					

INITIAL SCREENING

In the first conversation with a lender, they are typically trying to get a very brief overview of the business, equity fundraising history, the capital needs of the company, and expected time frame to put a financing package in place. Usually, these calls are with a relatively senior person at the firm and last thirty to forty-five minutes. The lender will ask a few questions; however, these initial calls are not meant to be in depth but an evaluation of whether to take the next step.

Depending on how a potential borrower was connected to a lender, there may not be an initial screening conversation at all. For example, if Sequoia, Greylock, A16Z, or any other brand-name venture capital firm recently led a new equity financing into the business and the same equity firm introduced that company to a lender, those lenders may jump straight to a full diligence process and skip the intro call. However, most of the time, lenders will want to have an initial screening call.

Although that initial conversation is short, most lenders, if they're good, are (1) trying to confirm whether the business and debt request fit in their wheelhouse or (2) if not, provide a quick "no" so they don't burn cycles for either party. It's both good reputation management and time management for a lender to say, *Hey, folks, this is not a commentary on your business, but for our lending philosophy, this isn't a perfect fit.* A good lender will also try to provide the company with a few other firms that might have interest, if any.

After that initial conversation, and assuming the lender wants to start doing real diligence, they will introduce additional members of their team or, occasionally, you may be handed off to a new team entirely. It really depends on how the bank or private credit firm is structured. At a private credit fund, where there are often fewer employees, that question might not be as important, but at a bank, there are hundreds of people who each cover a specific geography, sector, or stage. Once you have the right contact points, they will send over a diligence list to kick off the underwriting process.

THE DILIGENCE LIST

Most lenders want to see the same core set of documents with some variety around the edges. A common diligence list would include the following items:

- Company overview deck or investment pitch deck used during the last equity fundraise
- Annual and monthly historical financials going back two years (if the company has been around that long)
- Monthly or quarterly projections for the next eighteen to twenty-four months, including both income statement and balance sheet
- A/R and A/P agings from the prior three months if the company is already generating revenue
- Detailed cap table, including preferred shareholder and founder-level detail
- Articles of incorporation post the last equity fundraise
- Most recent 409a valuation

This list should be readily available if a company has completed an equity fundraise within the last twelve months. Most lenders are not trying to make a company create anything from scratch.

PRO TIP: What About a Non-Disclosure Agreement?

All lenders are willing to sign NDAs before gathering diligence. However, they will typically want to use their standard form NDA and are loath to negotiate the language. Is it possible to negotiate some of the language? Yes. Is it worth it? In my opinion, it is not. Just sign their standard form and move on. If you ever get to a point where you or the lender is pulling the signed NDA out of a drawer because someone feels they were wronged, the battle is already lost.

In fact, I'm not sure spending time on an NDA in the first place is worth it. Roughly 50% of the transactions I worked on in the prior two years did not have one in place. If a lender makes it a practice to share confidential info in the market, that will get around and they will lose credibility FAST. If your objective is to move quickly to get a debt structure in place, skipping the NDA will help shave anywhere from a couple of days to a few weeks off your process. But as usual, please consult your own outside counsel when making the decision.

Other items that might come up depending on the type of the company or a lender's particular sensitivities:

- Recurring revenue metrics (CAC, LTV, churn, etc.)
- Detailed customer pipeline
- Sample customer contracts
- Entity chart detailing corporate structure
- Flow of funds breakdown (for fintech, primarily)
- Quality of earnings report (later-stage, if available)
- FDA approval pipeline or status (for life science and healthcare companies)

Let's assume you get whatever is on the initial diligence list to the lender within a couple of days; how long will it take to hear back from that lender? Most firms will reply within a week to schedule a handful of in-person or video calls to cover questions that came up in their initial review. Lenders will want to be sure that they have a healthy understanding of the business to determine whether they want to present a financing proposal to their internal investment or credit committees. They may also occasionally ask to talk with your investors or board members ahead of issuing a formal term sheet. Investor diligence calls are normal, but most commonly happen after term sheet execution. Full detail on investor diligence by lenders is covered in Chapter 4. All this work is to ensure lenders can articulate what they've learned about the business and answer any number of questions that come from internal decision-makers. More on how banks and private credit funds are structured to come shortly.

The amount of documentation and depth of questioning you get from any given lender before they issue a term sheet will vary based on the sector and scale of the business. It will also differ based on how each lender thinks about the "finality" of their term sheets. Do they front load all their diligence to ensure they can honor anything they put on paper, or do they want to move quickly, get you a term sheet with the assumption that there could be changes (hopefully not material) upon further diligence down the road?

Reputation risk is a real thing. No lender wants to shoot themselves in the foot with a company and the broader market by issuing a term sheet they can't deliver on. So why does it still happen occasionally? Three reasons: (1) The lender is moving quickly to get a term sheet out and doesn't get all the information they wanted. After putting out initial terms, they discover that the company profile isn't as stellar as they thought and subsequently change the terms of their lending proposal. (2) A more junior member or less credible member of the lending team commits to the specifics of a term sheet but doesn't have full internal buyoff to do the deal, leading to changing the terms or passing altogether. (3) During further diligence, a lender discovers new information that truly does increase the risk of the transaction that forces a change in terms or the firm walking away altogether.

INDICATION OF INTEREST

Occasionally, a company will start providing diligence items to a lender and then the lender quickly shares an indication of interest ("IOI"); this may also be called the less formal "indicative terms." This will likely be one page or one slide outlining the key terms of a potential lending relationship. Usually, several of the terms in an IOI will have ranges or brackets or even TBDs listed. Why would a lender share this with a prospective borrower before a full-term sheet?

Three possible reasons: (1) This may be just their normal process when talking to potential portfolio companies. A lender may view this as a more collaborative way to work with a company that allows both parties to help shape the structure. (2) The company is great but the debt request may be just on the edge of a lender's comfort zone, perhaps at the upper end of the dollar amount they typically like to provide to any company, for example. In that situation, a lender may be sharing indicative terms to get an early reaction from the company about whether that lender's terms stand a chance of winning the company's business, assuming it is a competitive process. (3) The company is not as great and what they've asked the lender to provide is not easy. If the lender didn't already say "no" during initial screening, they may come back with indicative terms quickly to see if the company can swallow the structure and pricing of their potential deal. Regardless of the reason for sharing indicative terms, it is all an attempt by the lender to save time for both parties if not a fit.

PRO TIP: Is It a Term Sheet or Indication of Interest?

Confirm with your lender whether what you have in front of you is a full-blown term sheet or a less formal indication of interest that will be followed by a more detailed term sheet. Once you have term sheets in hand, ask each lender what amount of diligence happens after the term sheet? Whatever their answer, ask specifically again "How much diligence, if any, is left post term sheet to get to a fully approved transaction?" They can't always anticipate everything that may come up, but this should help avoid frustration on both sides post term sheet execution. I'd suggest factoring in the level of diligence needed following the term sheet as one of the decision-making criteria for who you chose to partner with.

THE TERM SHEET

At this point, you should have a decent idea of which firms are interested in lending your company money and who may be dragging their feet. After two to four weeks from the initial screening conversations, you should start to receive term sheets from the different firms you've engaged with. In Chapters 5 through 8, I walk through the specifics of a typical term sheet, section by section. If you'd like to dig in on those details, skip ahead; I won't be offended. To understand the rest of a typical venture debt process, read on.

AFTER THE TERM SHEET

Congratulations! You've selected your new lending partner and signed their term sheet. What now? After executing the term sheet, there are two parallel processes that kick off. The first is the lender's final diligence of the company and completing their internal approval. The internal approval is a gating item for the transaction to close. The second process is drafting, negotiating, and executing the definitive legal documents for the deal.

PRO TIP: Outside Counsel

Most lenders are willing to engage outside counsel to start drafting legal documents once they have a signed term sheet in hand. This helps save time while they finalize their diligence and approvals. There is a very small risk that they find something in their final diligence that scuttles a deal or for some reason the deal structure does not get approved by their investment committee. The odds of that happening are low, so ideally, confirm with your lender that they are willing to parallel path legal docs, because it will help shorten the overall time frame.

FINAL DILIGENCE AND INTERNAL APPROVAL

The work that your lender has done leading up to issuing their term sheet is what I would call exploratory due diligence. They are coming up the curve on the business from a standing start, asking lots of questions, and homing in on the key risks that they need to fully understand and underwrite. Post term sheet, a lender is mostly doing confirmatory due diligence on things they expect to come back fine or that are more of the check-the-box variety. Three categories of diligence commonly happen after the term sheet.

The first category is diligence calls with investors. Your lender will want to talk to several board members, typically from the firms with the largest ownership stake in the business, if they haven't already. What was the original thesis when they put money into the company? Expectations over the next twelve to twenty-four months? Areas of concern or things that aren't working right now? These are a smattering of the questions that may come up during these calls.

The second diligence item that comes up after the term sheet are customer reference calls. This is not requested all that often, but it does happen occasionally with mid-and later-stage companies that are putting a large strip of venture debt in place or if the company has a significant customer concentration. A lender may ask to talk to several customers to confirm how they feel about the product and/or service to date.

The last type of diligence that comes up post term sheet are questions that were raised during the lender's internal deliberation. These are commonly the bulk of the confirmatory diligence. The lender's investment committee may have asked about parts of the business that hadn't been covered in prior diligence. Or a topic was covered at a high enough level for a term sheet, but now the lender wants further detail. The lending team you are working with will come back to you to fill in those gaps.

Once confirmatory diligence is completed, the lender will take the proposed deal back to their investment committee (IC) or internal credit officer for final approval. The underwriting package for a new venture debt deal can range from 20–100 pages of material. This package is the formal record that documents the structure of the deal, the diligence done, the potential risks, and their mitigants. This is the main record that internal auditors or regulators may review in the future to confirm the lender is following their underwriting guidelines and policies. Time frames can vary based on availability of investors or customers for diligence calls and for a lender's internal approval processes, but a reasonable expectation is three to four weeks post term sheet execution to have internal approval completed.

PRO TIP: Keep an Eye on Time Lines

It is important to keep tabs on the internal approval process of your lender. Most of the time, it will be a nonevent, but if timelines start to slip or the process drags, you should be asking explicitly what the holdup is. That way, you can proactively help resolve the issue if needed. In the worst case, you can start rekindling discussions with other firms if the deal were to fall apart for whatever reason.

LEGAL DOCUMENTATION

Along with final diligence and approval, your lender engages outside counsel to draft the legal documents needed to memorialize the transaction. Almost all banks and private credit funds keep a roster of three to five different law firms they use depending on the size and complexity of a transaction. They will pick the right firm for the deal, clear conflicts (ensure the law firm isn't working with you or your investors already), and get to drafting documents. Every lender has their own unique legal document templates, but they largely have the same provisions throughout, with minor variation on the edges. It will take two to three weeks on average to get initial documents into the borrower's hands. This involves the initial drafting, the lender reviewing, and providing any commentary back to counsel on the draft before sharing broadly.

PRO TIP: Outside Counsel Costs

Ask your lender to get a legal quote from outside counsel to have an estimate of potential fees from their side. Then do your best to hold them accountable to that amount or at least ask them to proactively let you know when fees are reaching that level during negotiations.

Once legal documents make it to the company, they will share them with their outside counsel. This is where time frames can become hard to predict, because there are now four parties involved, two of which argue for a living and charge by the hour. Most legal negotiations take three to five turns (sending legal comments back and forth between parties) of the documents and run six to eight weeks. This assumes both parties are using experienced outside counsel and are all reasonable. As you can imagine though, the variance on those ranges can be wide and costs can quickly add up; it is a good reason to negotiate a legal cap, something we discuss in Chapter 6. If all parties are motivated and have a specific date or event they are working toward, processes can move faster than what I've outlined. More often though, legal negotiations can get bogged down and really drag out. I've seen a few transactions over my career unexpectedly take up to a year to complete. That. Was. Not. Fun. For. Anyone. If you are an entrepreneur, lender, lawyer, or investor reading this, don't let a deal drag on that long. Tips on how to run an efficient legal process from two great law firms are in Chapter 9, but for now, just do the inverse of what I outline in the next section.

THINGS THAT SLOW DOWN A VENTURE DEBT FUNDRAISE THAT AREN'T OBVIOUS

Here are three ways that I have seen companies inadvertently contribute to the slowdown of a venture debt fundraise.

Not having diligence items readily available. Don't start talking to lenders until you have the majority, if not all, of what I outlined in a standard diligence list, scrubbed and readily available. Do your best to have backup and supporting information available as well.

Talking to too many firms. You might think talking to as many lenders as possible is a way to get many different term sheets and thus somehow get a better deal. In my experience, the opposite ends up being true. Most lenders can tell if they are one of a few or one of many and adjust their response and effort accordingly. Having to manage that many lender conversations is also challenging for a company. My recommendation is to go to the right firms—three to five at most—to source venture debt options. This number allows you to put a decent amount of effort into each conversation without getting overly burdensome. If you get unfavorable responses from the initial subset of firms, expand your outreach from that point. Talking to more than one hand's worth of lenders at any given time is setting yourself up for unnecessary pain.

Internal counsel. Numerous companies I've worked with over the years have brought on a general counsel ("GC"). They tend to be great at helping the business navigate uncertainty of all types. Where they tend to be less great is when they decide to negotiate a venture debt agreement to save money on outside counsel. If the GC runs point, the venture debt process will go slower. It will also be more expensive, particularly when it gets bogged down and the GC finally brings in outside counsel to do cleanup. A GC doesn't know the standard legal terms and norms—they haven't done hundreds of deals in the past twelve months—they ask for things from lenders that are never going to get approved. Just don't do it. Use experienced outside counsel. For everyone's sake.

3

HOW BANKS AND PRIVATE CREDIT FUNDS ARE STRUCTURED

Within banks and private credit firms, four groups of people are generally involved in the underwriting, approval, and ongoing portfolio management of venture debt loans. Those groups are business development, relationship and portfolio managers, credit officers and investment committee members, and special assets. Depending on the size of the bank or the private credit fund, you may find people wearing multiple hats or performing multiple roles. Regardless of exactly how a firm is structured, it is helpful to know the role(s) the people you are engaged with hold within their firm and how that may impact decision-making now and in the future.

ORIGINATION AND BUSINESS DEVELOPMENT

People who work in loan origination or business development ("BD") have outward facing roles, and their core responsibility is to be out in the market building new relationships and sourcing new companies that need to borrow money. The BD people are the ones you will tend to see at events, shaking hands, and kissing babies. These folks typically focus on high lever points or high network nodes, like VCs, consulting finance firms, lawyers, and industry groups. They are hoping to be at or near the top of the list when an individual company or entrepreneur asks any one of those four groups, "Do you know a good venture lender?"

People get into the originator role in one of two ways depending on how a bank or private credit fund is structured. One way the role is filled is by very senior people who have done all the other jobs at the firm. By nature of having been around so long, they have a strong network already, a good personal brand in the innovation ecosystem, and are regularly sought out by others. As very senior people with deep connections, the thinking is that they will be able to be the rainmakers for their firm.

The other way into an originator role is, ironically, the polar opposite; you may find very junior people out in market. They may be extroverted, like to attend events, and have the energy to network like crazy. Those two types of people are probably going to approach BD very differently, but you have a barbell, if you will, where either it's senior people or it's junior people, maybe a combination of both, who are going to pursue new opportunities.

The originator roles are as close to an enterprise sales rep that you'll find because, while they are not paid fully on commission, most of their compensation comes from sourcing and originating new lending relationships for their institution. Originators are motivated to push hard to get deals done, given their compensation structure and the potential impact to their ongoing employment if they aren't sourcing enough new opportunities.

If you're an entrepreneur, you want to know where the people you're talking to sit within the structure of their organization. Maybe you're spending a lot of time as a founder or CFO talking to the sales or BD person. That's not a bad thing per se, but you want to explicitly ask this person whether they're going to hand you off at some point to someone else or another team entirely who will be managing the ongoing relationship. If so, you want to meet that person or team early in the process.

Companies should meet all the parties as opposed to just building their relationship with the origination person, who will walk out the door at some point, post-close, and you'll be stuck with people that you may not know as well. Not every firm has a pure BD role, but you should explicitly ask every person you meet where they sit within the firm and how they will be involved (or not) in the ongoing relationship.

RELATIONSHIP AND PORTFOLIO MANAGEMENT

These roles are where the bulk of the direct lending-related headcount of a bank or private credit fund sit and where I spent all my twenty plus years in the venture-lending world. Other groups that support direct lending efforts including great back-office people in operations, HR, marketing, and IT, but they don't interact directly with portfolio companies.

A relationship manager ("RM") is the primary point of contact between a lender and a portfolio company. At a bank, a relationship manager will work with a company whether they are borrowing money or only have treasury or deposit needs. The RM will be actively involved in the underwriting, structuring, and negotiation of any lending. They may do the initial screening call if there is no separate BD person involved. Depending on the bank or private credit fund, these people may not have RM in their title; you may see vice president ("VP"), senior vice president ("SVP"), director, principal, or managing director ("MD") on their LinkedIn profiles or email signatures. People with any of these titles are generally on the relationship management side of the house, but it's also good to confirm explicitly.

At some banks and private credit funds, the RM function does all the underwriting, structuring, negotiating, and ongoing portfolio management. At other banks and private credit funds, you may see a bifurcation. RMs will still be there as your primary point of contact and involved in the debt origination, but another group enters the discussions, sometimes called portfolio management ("PM") or credit solutions ("CS"). These folks are only involved with lending relationships. They help drive the underwriting, structuring, and negotiation of the initial transaction. Then, more often than not, they take a lead role in the ongoing portfolio management after the deal closes. Meaning they will be reviewing all the financial reporting, having update calls with the company, monitoring ongoing performance, etc.

Neither model is perfect. There are pros and cons to both. The caliber of the people involved, regardless of their function, is far more important. As an entrepreneur, you want to know the roles of all the people you are dealing with: Are they going to be involved for the duration of the relationship? Will they step out at some point? Are there other people who will step in? These are good questions to ask as you evaluate the firm you want to work with.

CREDIT OFFICERS AND INVESTMENT COMMITTEE MEMBERS

Now we come to the group of people who have the real power, the credit officers (CO)—at least in banks, where this role is very common. Every lender of any scale separates the deal origination, relationship, and portfolio management functions from the decision-maker role. It is usually required by regulators or limited partners but is also just good governance not to have the people tasked with evaluating and taking risk (i.e., originating new venture debt loans) to also be the ones deciding what is a good risk to take. COs provide that check and balance.

This group of people tend to be internally facing and typically don't interact directly with portfolio companies on a regular basis. They have the delegated authority of the institution to decide whether the institution will make a new loan, modify or change the terms of an existing loan, or change the risk designation of a particular loan. For most institutions in the United States who provide venture debt, these roles are filled with very senior people who have been lenders themselves, are excellent underwriters, understand portfolio construction, and are willing to say "no" when necessary.

Originators, RMs, and portfolio managers will all have regular dialogue with their credit officers about new transactions and the performance of existing portfolio companies. Those same externally facing people aggregate the firsthand information they have from a company combined with their own analysis or opinion when presenting to a credit officer. The credit officer then has two primary questions to answer: (1) Since everything is secondhand, do they trust the RM, PM, or originator's judgment and ability to ask all the right questions? (2) Given all the information they do have, is this a deal they are willing to approve?

PRO TIP: In-Person Meetings

If an entrepreneur can get an in-person meeting with a credit officer or investment committee member who will be one of the approvers of their new loan, this is good use of their time. Hearing a founder's vision firsthand speaks volumes. Although a good relationship manager can articulate the story of what a company is trying to do and can paint a picture of the people and their ideas, there is nothing like hearing it firsthand. A meeting with a credit officer allows them to ask questions they might not otherwise have a chance to cover. They often will get excited about a new technology or business. Everyone in venture lending loves to hear about something new that a company is building. Often, the founder's passion and commitment are contagious. If you have the chance, get in front of a credit officer and tell your story. It doesn't guarantee a good deal, but I'd be willing to wager that you will get more flexibility from that lender having done so.

Every lender has a formal credit policy of how they approve or modify loans to their portfolio companies. They also have a formal policy that lays out how they evaluate and rate the riskiness of any company at a given point in time called a "risk rating." Some lenders, mostly banks, have different levels of approval authority vested in their credit officers. Depending on the size of the transaction—itself a measurement of risk—and the actual risk rating, one or multiple credit officers may need to be involved in the ultimate decision and approval. I've created a mocked up delegated authority matrix that outlines what this might look like. As dollar size or risk increase, more people get involved.

		Amount		
		$	$$	$$$
Risk Rating	Lower Risk	Credit Officer Only	Credit Officer Only	Credit Officer + Senior Credit Officer
	Moderate Risk	Credit Officer Only	Credit Officer + Senior Credit Officer	Credit Officer + Senior Credit Officer + Chief Credit Officer
	High Risk	Credit Officer + Senior Credit Officer	Credit Officer + Senior Credit Officer + Chief Credit Officer	All credit roles + CEO/President

A few banks and almost all private credit funds use an investment or credit committee model to review and approve all their transactions. Why? Private credit funds don't have the deal flow volume to necessitate a delegated authority model and like to have their most senior partners review each new transaction, given their typical size. This looks like what a lot of VC firms do within their partnership, collectively voting to approve new investments. A committee model for a bank or fund means there is a standing meeting each week where a group of two to three very senior members of the firm review and approve new transactions. The lending team talking to the company presents the proposed deal and fields any questions the committee may have. The upside of this model is that you don't have to navigate a matrix like what I outlined above since every deal goes to the committee. The downside is that it can add incremental delays to a process because a committee can only handle a certain number of transactions during a meeting, and if the agenda is full, a deal discussion may get bumped out a week or more.

SPECIAL ASSETS, SPECIAL LOANS, ADVISORY SERVICES, OR THE WORKOUT GROUP

These are the people who as an entrepreneur, CFO, or investor, you hope you never have to meet. Not because they are bad humans or terrible to work with, but because this means your company is underperforming and possibly on life support. Every lender has a specialist or a full team focused on distressed situations. These individuals or teams will have a variety of potential names. Several of them include the less exciting version of the word "special," and it generally means you are going to receive a lot of attention from these groups.

Why do lenders want separate teams to get involved when companies are having trouble? Wouldn't it be better to have continuity of relationship and let the existing RMs or portfolio managers navigate the situation? Sometimes that can make sense for a lender, but a lot of the time, it doesn't work. There are three primary reasons for a separate team or individual to join or take over a relationship with a portfolio company having trouble: (1) Expertise. If a company is truly headed toward a wind down (bankruptcy, asset sale, or assignment for benefit of creditors), there is a lot of detail and nuance involved in those processes. While not rocket science, if you don't regularly live in that world, the odds that a normal lender will misstep or hamper a process are high. (2) Time. When a company is truly going sideways, the amount of time spent with the various players (company, board, investment bank running a sale process, court visits) is substantial. Weekly, if not daily, calls with the company are the norm and deadlines to make decisions are tight. Combine that new workload with the normal cadence of managing twenty to thirty other portfolio companies and you have a recipe for failure, burnout, or both. (3) Decision-making clarity. Having a relationship with the founding team, CFO, or investors is helpful in most situations. However, when hard choices and decisions need to be made, it can become a hindrance. It's hard to deliver tough news to people you know well and like. A fresh perspective and a degree of detachment can be helpful in a scenario where a company is really in trouble.

With private credit funds, you may see more of the original relationship team involved when a portfolio company goes sideways. Funds have fewer people in general, which means more folks wear multiple hats. But often, a new team will come in and take over when a company's situation meaningfully deteriorates.

PRO TIP: Continuing Relationships

Having said all that, the best relationship managers at banks or private credit funds try hard to stay involved, even if they have no official decision-making authority going forward. They can help influence decision-making within their firm in the background or, at a minimum, make sure everyone has the correct context and history for the relationship. My experience over the years has been that if the original relationship team stays involved, even if on the periphery, the company and investors at least appreciate the continuity. I've also found that the odds of a better outcome or softer landing increase in those situations. If you are a lender, do your best to stay engaged with these companies. If you are a founder, do your best to keep your original relationship team involved.

In regular commercial banking land, when the workout group gets involved in a relationship, it tends to signal the end of that company's time with that lender. The team is called the workout group because it is their job to work you out of the bank or fund. Three cheers for literal group names. In the innovation economy, things are more nuanced. The ecosystem is very interconnected, people understand that start-ups can be very dynamic, and everyone generally knows that the default outcome in Start-Up Land is likely failure. Many portfolio companies of mine have navigated near-death experiences and survived to tell the tale. Sometimes I was driving the relationship throughout, in other cases, my advisory services colleagues were involved or fully in charge. The best lenders work with their portfolio companies and their investors to find a good outcome for all parties, not just selfishly doing whatever they can to get repaid. Other lenders may not be so accommodating and act earlier to protect their capital.

PRO TIP: Who are Your Potential Lending Partners

Entrepreneurs should always do reference checks on potential lending partners: What is the firm's reputation and how have they navigated downside situations in the past? How do you find this out? You can ask a lender for references, but that will always lead to people who are likely to say good things. The most useful paths to get unvarnished feedback on a lender are to talk with your board, your outside counsel, and ask your CFO (if you have one) to canvas fellow CFOs in their network. You might also look at the portfolio companies referenced on a lender's website and reach out directly to the CEO/CFO through your own network.

4

HOW LENDERS EVALUATE COMPANIES

Lenders break the world of potential portfolio companies into two buckets. Early-stage companies that have raised a large seed or Series A, and mid- to later-stage companies that are Series B and beyond. Yes, there will be some gray area in the middle; yes, every company has unique characteristics; and yes, this is a broad generalization. But this will hold directionally correct for most situations.

Lenders to early-stage companies, which today are mostly venture banks and a small number of funds, aren't usually scouring the land-scape trying to find the next Nvidia, Stripe, or SpaceX. We covered earlier how most venture banks use their early-stage venture lending as quasi-customer acquisition financing. Knowing that, early-stage lenders are really evaluating the likelihood that a Series A company will successfully raise another round of equity. This is a different question than whether they can become the next world-changing company. Later-stage venture debt lenders, mostly private credit funds and a few banks, are more likely to be evaluating companies on whether they truly are best in class or are likely on a trajectory to have a good outcome, whether it be M&A or IPO. Some of the bank venture lenders also care about this for a different reason; their institution may have an investment banking arm. The potential to participate or lead an IPO or M&A process can be a strong motivator for those institutions. All lenders will spend time thinking about the diligence areas outlined in this chapter, but depending on the stage of the company, the questions or amount of depth from any individual firm will vary.

SOURCES OF REPAYMENT

No discussion about lending and underwriting would be complete without talking about sources of repayment. Lenders of all shapes and sizes are constantly thinking about the different ways that their debt can be repaid. They spend large chunks of time doing diligence on sources of repayment, then documenting that work in formal credit approvals. Auditors and regulators also review what lenders have called out as potential sources of repayment, then opine on whether they agree with the lender's assessment.

Almost all commercial lenders are hoping to have at least three potential sources of repayment from each of their borrowers: The primary source of repayment (PSOR), the secondary source of repayment (SSOR), and the tertiary source of repayment (TSOR). Finance people have a special love affair with acronyms. For most commercial banks around the world, sources of repayment from a normal business would usually be the following:

1. Cash flow from operations (PSOR)

2. Assets on the balance sheet (SSOR)

3. Sale of the business or personal guarantee of executives (TSOR)

Sometimes cash flow and assets on the balance sheet might swap places, particularly if a loan is specifically tied to a particular asset. But otherwise, you would see these three sources of repayment regularly across commercial lenders. Venture lenders are no different in looking for three sources of repayment from their borrowers. They are however evaluating different sources. For a venture debt loan, sources of repayment are usually as follows:

1. Cash proceeds from future equity financings (PSOR)

2. Assets on the balance sheet (SSOR)

3. Sale of the business or Intellectual Property (TSOR)

As a venture-backed company gets to significant scale, you might see assets on the balance sheet move up to be the PSOR, and if a company is one of the rare unicorns to achieve actual profitability, cash flow from operations will show back up on this list.

Why am I badgering you with internal lender underwriting policy and acronyms? Because it guides where venture lenders focus their diligence efforts and explains why they spend so much time focused on a company's cap table, sometimes spending the same time—if not more—than on the business itself. Speaking of which . . .

THE CAP TABLE

Since this is the primary source of repayment for most venture debt deals, lenders will want to know who the largest outside shareholders are and whether those firms have the capacity to continue supporting the company. The ideal situation is to have two or more well-known venture firms involved with the company. Even better is if the lender has worked with those venture firms in the past through good and bad times. Lenders will look to see if the vintage year of the major investor's funds are within the last three to four years—a good proxy for whether those funds should have meaningful callable capital available. If the funds are more dated, meaning eight to ten years old, lenders will have a harder time believing a fund can continue to support the company if needed.

Across the various equity rounds raised, has valuation been up and to the right throughout? That is ideal. A flat or down round will spark meaningful discussion with your lender to understand the backstory. Is the equity structure clean? Meaning 1× liquidation preference and non-participating preferred stock for all outside investors with no other off-market terms in the equity stack. This is what you would call a "clean" cap table and is what lenders want to see. Any variation from a clean equity structure will spark a variety of questions and will take more effort to get lenders comfortable with the company's ability to raise additional capital if needed.

The cap table will be a focus whether you are an early- or later-stage company, but the equity fundraising and history is an even more meaningful component of early-stage lending and mostly driven by the fact that early-stage companies have less financial performance to evaluate and comparisons to other more established businesses aren't all that useful.

INVESTOR DILIGENCE CALLS

Lenders will look at a cap table, articles of incorporation, 409a valuations, publicly available information online, and their own proprietary data to form an opinion on whether an individual investor or an entire cap table has the ability and willingness to support a company. But that is only part of the story. A key component of any venture lender's diligence process is talking directly with investors. They will want to talk to up to three board members, including the largest shareholder, and the firm that led the most recent equity financing.

The timing of investor diligence calls will vary, sometimes happening before a term sheet is issued, but more often happening after the term sheet is executed. The most valuable time frame from a lender's perspective is to have investor calls before the term sheet has been shared with a company. That allows the lender to incorporate what they hear from the various board members into the structure and pricing of the debt they want to propose.

Understandably, companies tend to try to keep lenders from talking to investors before a term sheet has been signed. That saves time for their investors because they don't have to talk to multiple potential lenders as opposed to just one if done after term sheet execution. Sometimes, an executive team will want to see terms from lenders to gauge whether they are even in the ballpark before allowing investor calls. And occasionally, a company hasn't informed the board they are evaluating venture debt options and so are trying to avoid catching board members off guard.

Regardless of the timing of investor diligence calls, what are lenders going to cover during these conversations? Usually, a mix of the following topics:

- Original investment thesis
- Key milestones and capital needs of the business over the next 12–18 months
- How the company's performance has tracked relative to expectations
- Competitive landscape
- What keeps the investor "up at night"?
- Follow-on investment capacity or reserves in the fund

The problem with the list above and with most investor diligence calls is that this process can very quickly become formulaic. Over the years, I've heard repeatedly from investors that a lender sounds robotic and is just checking off a list of items, which makes a lot of investors not very excited to talk to most lenders. Allow me to give both parties a few pointers.

For my fellow lenders: Do your best to have your own thesis for why your new portfolio company is going to succeed, as well as the issues they may face. Do your best to quickly articulate that to an investor and ask them to poke holes in that thesis, or to add on where they may agree. Doing this well means your prep will be two to three times longer than the call itself. Direct questions about callable capital or reserves for a company from an investor tend not to get answered explicitly. Better to ask about whether the fund expects to add new portfolio companies going forward (i.e., they have a sizable amount of capital left) or to confirm the vintage year and original amount of the fund. Then, you can likely do the math on potential reserves.

For the investor community: If I'm lucky enough to have you reading this book, a diligence call is your opportunity to get your portfolio company's lender more comfortable (or not) with the risk they are taking. Don't waste it. Experienced lenders can tell when you aren't giving them the full picture or when you don't know the details of a particular company. Do your best to come prepared. The effort you put in now and the relationship you build with that lender will pay off when your portfolio company needs flexibility for any number of reasons in the future.

I'm now off my "how to make investor diligence calls better" soapbox. Outside of the origination of a new venture debt loan, how often will these investor calls take place? Your lender will likely be talking to your investors at least annually, assuming no other reason to talk more frequently. Ideally, they will give you a heads-up beforehand. As a company goes into an equity fundraise process and by extension has lower liquidity, the frequency of those investor calls will increase to quarterly, monthly, or even weekly, depending on how the lender is feeling about the likelihood of a successful equity fundraise.

FINANCIALS AND KPIS

Regardless of the size, complexity, or history of the business, at some point every lender will want to do a line-by-line walk through of the financial statements. Balance sheet and income statement for sure, cash flow statement if they are thorough. If a company has millions of dollars in revenue and ramping, all three statements will be required. What is the definition of each line item, even if relatively obvious? Anything out of the ordinary like a loan to shareholders or employees or intangibles on the balance sheet will spark questions. If not covered already, lenders will ask for a walk through of the business model and product line(s), plus the revenue recognition standard being used for each. A detailed look at what is in COGS and how gross margin is calculated will also come up.

Lenders will look at historical performance, if there is any, and how that is tracking relative to other portfolio companies of a similar size. But most of the time will be spent looking at a company's forecast. The running joke among lenders is that the only thing you know for certain about a company's forecast is that it's wrong. So, most of the conversation will be about the assumptions and thinking behind the model. Can the founder or CFO credibly explain what drove the forecast? How many customers are assumed in the revenue ramp? Split between new and upsizing existing? Why are margins expanding, and how does that track to historical performance? What kind of sales org and pipeline coverage is needed to achieve this forecast? What are the critical milestones the company need to attain to successfully raise the next equity round? These are some of the many questions that will come up in diligence of a company's forecast. As a company scales, the forecast will take on more weight during underwriting because the business should, over time, become more predictable.

Each market niche (enterprise SaaS, e-commerce, AI, hard tech) usually has metrics specific to their type of business. Lenders will dig into those metrics because they want to understand how they are calculated (ARR means something different depending on who you ask) and the overall trendlines.

PRO TIP: Business Models and Assumptions

Most companies have put together several different models for the business using different types of assumptions. Something like the base case, upside, and downside is common. When talking with lenders, be sure to share every version of the model and the underlying assumptions. Lenders will come to their own conclusions about what they think is truly achievable, but you should guide them to underwrite a combination of the base case and downside model. What you are trying to avoid, and I discuss at length later in the book, is over-promising and under-delivering. Almost every start-up underperforms their plan, but you really want to avoid a wild swing and miss. That has the potential to spook a lender and, depending on the firm, might cause a harsher than expected reaction.

MARKET COMPS, VERTICAL, AND COMPETITIVE LANDSCAPE

For later-stage companies looking to bring on debt capital, lenders will be looking at similar private and public companies and how your company compares. This will include metrics like growth rate, gross margin, revenue to total equity raised, revenue multiple to current valuation, and more. Early-stage companies don't usually have enough time in business to make for meaningful market comps.

Lenders will look at the competitive landscape. Having competitors, even well-known ones, is not a bad thing. Most lenders expect competition, either from old-line companies using legacy tech or from other newly minted start-ups. They also expect the slide deck to show the company they are evaluating in the top right quadrant. Self-awareness be damned. A lot of the time, reviewing the competitive landscape helps a lender understand a company's go-to-market strategy better. It also creates a basket of competitors that the lender can track, along with the portfolio company, over time.

TEAM

This is a significant area of focus for equity investors, but frankly, this isn't nearly as big for most lenders. In large part because the lender is trusting the investors involved to have already done a certain level of diligence on the founding team. Most lenders don't have a deeply technical background, so they lack the ability (assuming they are self-aware) to diligence a founder or founding team's skill set. And these days, successful companies have been founded by nineteen-year-old college dropouts and older gray-haired types, so you can't really filter on demographics either. Lenders are evaluating whether a founder or CEO has the energy, passion, and the leadership skills to drive the business. A lot of that comes from pattern recognition by experienced lenders who've worked with other successful founding teams. Does this new founder or CEO size up to that level? Probably the biggest impact a team will have on a lender's willingness to provide capital at favorable terms is whether the team is made up of repeat founders. Better yet, repeat founders the lender worked with previously. Otherwise, diligence on the team tends to be closer to a check-the-box exercise.

INTANGIBLES

Pattern recognition is a big one here. Lenders, like VCs, talk with hundreds of companies and entrepreneurs every year. They have a feel for what a "normal" start-up looks like and when something is out of pattern or "abnormal." That can be good or bad depending on the situation. When a lender visits a company in person, they get a feel for the office culture or vibe, even post-COVID. *Is there a lot of energy in the place or does it feel like a morgue? How do the CEO, founders, and rest of the executive team get along? Is there a sense of pent-up frustration or tension between colleagues during group conversations?* It happens more than you would think.

THIS IS ART, NOT SCIENCE

There are some hard rules and guidelines that underpin each lender's underwriting philosophy and risk tolerance, but that does not mean that venture lenders are formulaic. Each company and the people involved are different. The circumstances are unique. The market is always moving. The lender itself is changing its viewpoint regularly—which is all a way of saying that I can't pin down for you exactly how any lender will approach a given situation. The correct answer is generally . . . it depends.

CASE STUDY

NO (AIR)MATTRESSES WERE HARMED
IN THE MAKING OF THIS FILM—AIRBNB

"I NEED A LOAN! . . . *I NEED A LOAN!*" a man screamed into the phone. This is what an average call to the 800 number at SVB sounded like. A loud voice on the other end of the phone, not making any sense or asking for something that we couldn't provide. When I started at SVB in 2009, there was a role called the "officer of the day." This was somebody from a lending team, usually a junior member, who was on call to help the customer service team or office admins when somebody called the 800 number and wanted to know about SVB's products or services, particularly lending. The officer of the day wouldn't field every call on that 800 number, just the ones that required more expertise.

Today, there is probably an AI bot that will have that conversation, but in 2009, it was an actual person. Typically, the calls were odd because anybody in the innovation economy would likely know somebody at SVB, or they would get a warm intro to SVB from someone else in their network. So, 99% of the time, calls to the 800 number were from somebody who wanted to finance farm vehicles, for example, or coffee in Yemen, or just a crazy person incoherently yelling at the top of their lungs. No offense to farmers, coffee from Yemen (which is quite good, actually), or crazy people around the world, but this made being officer of the day a thankless job that was usually met with a groan.

In mid-2009, a call came into the officer of that particular day, a fine gentlemen named Matt Trotter, and the guy on the phone said to him, in a calm voice, thankfully, "We are a newly minted start-up that just went through Y Combinator, and we'd like to open an account with SVB." Matt asked about the business model and got a vague answer about becoming an online bed-and-breakfast. While not the *most* off-the-wall thing Matt had ever heard since he had been officer of the day numerous times already, it still didn't sound promising or likely a business SVB would be able to help, at least not at this stage. Like most humans at the time, he didn't think anyone was going to want to rent a cheap inflatable mattress in an apartment with several other random people. But the guy on the phone said they'd raised a small amount of money from investors (TBD), so Matt decided it was at least worth the time to go out and meet the founders. He and another colleague headed out to an apartment in the SOMA area of San Francisco and met the three founders of the company—who were in their pajamas with four or five air mattresses strewn about the place. That might be a more common situation these days or certainly in the show *Silicon Valley*, but in 2009, this was not the norm. Matt politely listened to them describe the business, and while SVB had prided itself on being "willing to suspend disbelief" for years, Matt was on the verge of saying it wasn't a great fit for the bank when the CEO mentioned their initial investment was from Sequoia Capital. That CEO was Brian Chesky, and the company was Airbnb.

Sequoia Capital is one of the top venture firms on the planet, and SVB had a long history of working with the firm. Further social proof with the check from Sequoia and the company being a part of the winter 2009 Y Combinator batch was enough to convince Matt that this company was worth bringing into the banking portfolio at SVB. I ended up as the beneficiary of his fateful decision when, after a reshuffling of teams within SVB (a common occurrence), yours truly took over the Airbnb relationship mid-2011. It was a seamless handoff since we look essentially the same—athletic, bearded, and balding, yet still ruggedly handsome. It also helps that we share a lot of the same hobbies and are good friends to this day.

After taking over as the relationship manager for Airbnb, I didn't immediately interact much with the business because they didn't have any needs. We knew the business was growing rapidly, that it had started to build a very loyal customer base, and it had raised a new equity round that saw the company become one of the first "unicorns" back when that wasn't really a thing. Everything we knew about the company was largely from what was covered by the tech press. That changed in early 2012 when we got a call from the fractional CFO working with them, Bill Gerth, who said they might need to borrow some money.

In addition to understanding what a company is trying to build, digging into its business model, and evaluating the investors on the cap table, lenders are also looking at a few more basic things. A couple of those come from visiting a company in person, which I and a colleague did at Airbnb's Rhode Island Street headquarters in San Francisco in the middle of 2012. First item to check off that is really at a Lending 101 level: Is there a real office and are there real people there? Essentially, you are checking for a certain type of fraud. Airbnb, given the company profile and investors involved, was *very* unlikely to be a candidate for fraud. But stranger things have happened and the prevalence of fake businesses that seemed real has stepped up significantly over the years, particularly post-COVID.

The company passed the quick fraud check easily, as expected. The next thing on a lender's list during an in-person meeting is a pulse check of the energy in the office. Are there a lot of employees around? Do they seem happy to be there? Energetic? Excited? Or does it feel like a prison, a mortuary, or the cube farm in *Office Space*? Airbnb is the first company I can think of in my career where I walked into their office and it was radiating with the energy of people who seemed to just be stoked to be building the product and business. It's almost hard to describe what it felt like, but there were just a ton of happy people around the office. I'm sure this was partly because Airbnb was in the early innings of a rocket ship ride to becoming a category-defining company, but also partly due to an impressive company culture the founders seemed to have built.

The company was growing its headcount rapidly and wanted to expand to a new office in the SoMa area of San Francisco, 888 Brannan Street to be precise. The landlord of the building wanted a security deposit from Airbnb, in this case a significant amount: $9,000,000.

PRO TIP: Security Deposits

Don't ever give a landlord a security deposit in cash. There are some great landlords out there and some that are not so great. I've seen numerous landlords mysteriously "lose" a security deposit. Worse still, the landlord goes out of business and the deposit is truly gone. The best way to handle a security deposit is to set up a letter of credit ("LC") with a bank in favor of the landlord. The bank sets aside the same amount of your cash and then provides a promise to pay the landlord if you don't meet your obligations under the lease. Even though you still must set aside cash, it is sitting at your bank and not with your landlord, limiting the risk of it being "lost."

Airbnb was smart enough to do just that, and they were asking us to provide a $9,000,000 LC to their new landlord. However, they did not want to set aside their own cash to secure the LC and so wanted us to provide it without that requirement. They also wanted to make significant improvements prior to moving into the building totaling $10,000,000, which they wanted to finance. In total, Airbnb wanted to borrow just under $20,000,000. While it had significant cash from its recent equity fundraising, it understandably didn't want to use a large portion of its equity dollars to secure and build out the new space.

I was sitting in an impressive replica of an English countryside tearoom as Airbnb's part-time CFO (Bill) and full-time controller (Stan Kong) explained why they wanted to borrow the money. Airbnb had turned their five main conference rooms into replicas of the top five rental properties on the platform at the time. Lenders half-jokingly evaluate a start-up by the quality of their office furniture, usually on an inverse scale; beat up and mismatched furniture means the company is scrappy and focused on executing. Fancy digs with new Aeron chairs at every desk meant the company cared more about appearance and spent on things that didn't really "matter." While Airbnb was closer to the fancy end of the scale, I was willing to give them a pass because it was a neat way to contextualize the experiences they were offering their users. And their performance justified it.

Bill and Stan gave us a quick overview of the business performance and financials at that initial meeting. I don't recall the specifics, but it was one of the best examples I've seen of revenue truly going "up and to the right." Yes, the business was burning a ton of cash, but I'd candidly never seen a business that was ramping as quickly as Airbnb, which was important because the amount of money they had asked to borrow would be the largest single venture debt commitment from SVB in its history at that time.

We agreed to another meeting to get a full overview of the business and the strategic road map for the next twelve to eighteen months. I asked for one of the founders to join that discussion. There are some truly great finance people out there who know the ins and outs of a business cold, but you can't replicate hearing directly from a founder or CEO about what they want to build. Bill and Stan had no issue with that and nicely asked Joe Gebbia to join. Knowing this financing request would get meaningful scrutiny inside SVB given its size, I asked one of our most senior credit people, Peter Kidder, to join as well. I needed to get him on board to help advocate internally in the hopes of getting approval to do the deal.

Our big meeting with Joe and Peter was in a nice but sadly run-of-the-mill conference room. Most of the time was spent listening to Joe cover recent performance of the business and Airbnb's strategic road-map. A few of the more memorable moments included Joe describing the now-famous story of how the founders sold Obama O's and Cap'n McCain's cereal boxes at the 2008 political conventions as a novel way to help fund the business early on. He told us about the importance of excellent photographs to help tell the story of each listing. How the founders had gone to personally take better pictures of some early listings and now had a roster of professional photographers to deploy around the world. He showed us how they could predict growth in the business. For example, when first-time users experienced an Airbnb, more than 20% (I can't recall the exact number—this is my best guess, forgive me) of the time they would go home and sign up to be a host in their home state or country. The Airbnb team could look at this ping-pong map around the world of people being guests and then becoming hosts that allowed them to be more predictive about the business. It was such a unique concept: providing people with the ability to stay in a local place, in someone's home, meet a local host, and avoid the sterile hotel that's downtown and not in the real "city" you wanted to visit.

Peter and I, plus the rest of my team, left that meeting inspired. Joe was an impressive storyteller. The business was jamming. The investors involved were top-notch. We had everything we needed to present the opportunity internally. Even with all that, it was still not a slam dunk. The dollar amount they wanted from us might just be too much risk to take, even with the profile of the company, at least for SVB at the time. Several other private credit funds were vying for the business. Those funds tend to play where banks tap out. While banks can provide north of $20M of venture debt these days, more than a decade ago, this was not common.

We were set to present the opportunity to our credit committee later that week. This standing meeting was where the largest or most risky lending opportunities for the bank were discussed, then approved or denied. A rotating group of senior SVB execs were voting members with one consistent standing member, SVB's chief credit officer, who was responsible for the entire loan portfolio of the bank and the risk that it represents. Getting him to a "yes" on any deal was never guaranteed. He had a reputation for being direct, tough, but thankfully, fair.

I led the presentation to our credit committee, outlining what we saw as the strengths and weaknesses in the business. How we viewed this company as truly exceptional at the time and that we thought this would likely be our only opportunity to provide debt to the business. After a variety of questions from the rotating members, it was time for our chief credit officer's questions . . . which were surprisingly few. It quickly went to a vote and the transaction was approved. A bit anticlimactic really. I'm a pretty good presenter and understood the business well, but even a blind monkey could figure out that Airbnb was doing great. Peter and I were both well-respected lenders, but that only gets you so far. So, what made this discussion so easy? As it turned out, our chief credit officer and his wife had several dogs they liked to travel with. He very quickly saw that Airbnb could be a great service to find houses that were pet-friendly around the country. I love dogs.

So off I went to present our $20M term sheet to the company. We were the only bank in the running that could provide both venture debt of that size and the letter of credit. There were other banks that could provide the LC and private credit funds who could provide the venture debt, but nobody else could do both. But there was still plenty of negotiating to be done. The private credit funds were more expensive than us, but they were also offering Airbnb more capital, in some cases, significantly more. While the company hadn't asked for the larger-dollar term sheets, they weren't opposed to evaluating the options. Over a month of back-and-forth with the company, it became clear we had two main advantages. One was the overall relationship we had built with Bill, Stan, and the rest of the team at Airbnb. We had been their primary bank for years and were a known quantity. I think we were also the least transactional lender they were evaluating because of the broader ongoing relationship. (Helpful that I had just learned a hard lesson about being transactional with the Socialcam spinout from Twitch, which happened the same year.)

Our second advantage was pricing. We were willing to provide our debt at a significantly lower cost than the private credit fund options Airbnb had in hand. Part of that was structural, as banks generally have a lower cost of funds (deposits) plus an ongoing banking relationship to monetize. Private credit funds must raise money from third parties and don't have the benefit of a broader relationship. We were also willing to trade off a portion of our warrants for a direct "right to invest" in the business. The company felt better about that mix because a warrant is typically just granted to the lender with no cash exchanged; a right to invest meant the company would get cash and SVB would take the terms of the next equity financing. A good trade. Last, we were willing to be overly accommodating to Airbnb because of the profile of the business. Winning the lending relationship with the company, one of the earliest unicorns and highest profile companies in Silicon Valley, had significant marketing value to SVB at the time.

We received the signed term sheet while I was on a ski trip in Colorado with my girlfriend (now wife) who, thankfully, tolerated me repeatedly delaying our ski days to field a variety of last-minute calls to seal the deal. It felt great to carry the day with such a high-profile business and was made even better given the relationship we had already built with the people there.

AFTERMATH

Funny enough, after all that, the company never drew down the venture debt because it raised a huge preemptive equity round in 2013 and didn't look back. They used our letter of credit to secure the 888 Brannan lease, and we continued to be their banking partner for years, but they never borrowed from SVB again. However, much later, the company needed to borrow again from the private credit world as the early impact of COVID looked like it might scuttle the entire Airbnb business. In the first half of 2020, the company struck a deal for $1B from Silver Lake and Sixth Street, two of the largest private credit funds in the business. That costly capital gave the lenders a 1% equity stake in the business. It was quickly refinanced as the market rebounded off its lows in May 2020 and remote work became a demand driver for Airbnb. In what was likely an incredibly stressful year for the company, they ended up going public in December 2020. They remain an impressive founder-led business to this day. The warrant we held in the company and the equity dollars we invested drove significant returns, well over the debt capital we committed to the business.

KEY TAKEAWAYS

Spending time with the right lender, educating them, and being available to them pays dividends. I've been fortunate to talk with thousands of founders and investors over my venture-lending career. A lot of the people in those two groups were a delight to work with. However, some companies and founders make the mistake of thinking of lenders purely as service providers. They will give the lenders the bare minimum of diligence information and expect to see amazing options to borrow money. If a lender has been talking with a CFO or the finance team then asks to have a full company overview with the founder or CEO, they may be told no or that they need to "earn" the right to talk to the founder/CEO after sending across worthwhile terms. A lender may get in front of the founders, then quickly get the sense they think this whole meeting is a waste of time. All these situations come up because start-up execs and founders can have healthy egos. Sometimes that ego is very justified, the company is truly hot shit, but I've found that a lot of times, it is not.

I would not have been surprised to find healthy egos among the executives and founders of the Airbnb team. It would have been well earned because their company was a rocket ship. To their credit, though, the opposite was true. The finance team, led by Bill and Stan, were an open book. They were willing to answer questions whenever needed, willing to take the time to help us understand the business. They didn't balk when we asked to have one of the founders give us an overview of the business. Joe Gebbia couldn't have been more fun to talk with. Similarly, he was willing to answer any question we threw at him. The company was also happy to have us talk to investors as part of our diligence process ahead of putting out a term sheet. For one of the best companies built in the last twenty years, they were all surprisingly humble.

The practical benefit to Airbnb's humility was that they were able to get a flexible, relatively inexpensive piece of debt capital that, unbeknownst to them, was the largest venture debt transaction for SVB to date. My team and I were even more motivated to help whenever the company needed anything going forward because we knew the whole team well and they were a delight to work with. Stan Kong and I continue to be friends almost fifteen years later. Airbnb is a good example of the kind of relationship you should strive to build with your lender if/when you decide to borrow money.

Having a credit or investment committee member join diligence meetings is generally a good thing. Peter Kidder joining our big diligence meeting was an important component of getting the deal approved internally. While I was the one who had the idea, the company didn't have an issue with a new face joining the conversation. If you are evaluating venture lenders, confirming who will be making the ultimate decision on the transaction and seeing whether one or more of those voting members can join a diligence meeting may be well worth the time.

Understand the motivations of the lenders in the mix. I talked to a managing director at a private credit fund who competed against us on the Airbnb opportunity shortly after we closed our deal with the company. He was bummed to lose, congratulated me on the win, and then went on to say he thought we had severely underpriced our deal for the risk we were taking. At the time I laughed it off, but to be honest, we *had* underpriced the deal; we had other motivations. The marketing value of having Airbnb in the portfolio was very impactful at the time. The right to invest we secured and then exercised when the company raised its Series C in 2013 had a twofold impact. It turned out to be a great economic return when the company went public in 2020, and it helped SVB Capital (the equity investing practice at SVB at the time, now a stand-alone group as part of Pinegrove Capital Partners) demonstrate their continued ability to source and invest in breakout companies across the innovation ecosystem. Arguably, the Airbnb investment helped our SVB Capital team raise its next direct equity fund. It is important for you, as an entrepreneur, to understand the motivations behind each party you are talking to when evaluating lenders. Some motivations may be obvious. A lot will be similar. But you never know what you might uncover, possibly to your benefit.

5

OVERVIEW AND STRUCTURAL COMPONENTS OF THE TERM SHEET

Over my twenty-year venture lending career, I've drafted hundreds of term sheets and reviewed thousands of others from SVB and from most venture banks and private credit funds in the business. They tend to all cover the same major points with some variety in the level of detail and presentation style. Over the next four chapters, I'll break down—in what I hope is only *somewhat* excruciating detail—what each line item in a term sheet means, what lenders are usually thinking about in the background, and what an entrepreneur or company should consider when negotiating. Before we jump into the nitty-gritty, a few overarching comments:

- In Appendix 1 and 2, you'll find sample term sheets for both an early- and later-stage profile company. The early-stage example is more like what you will see from a venture bank; the later-stage example mirrors what you would more commonly see from a private credit fund. It may help to reference the appendices as you read through this section, or if you are the lucky recipient of actual term sheets from actual lenders, bring them up on screen or print them out and read along.

- Assuming a lender has been willing to provide a term sheet in the first place, there will be plenty of back-and-forth before signing. There is a lot of interplay between size of the debt commitment, structure, and economics. None of these changes happen independently of each other, and if a lender gives you additional flexibility in one area, another area may change. Sometimes that movement will be inversely correlated, i.e., the commitment amount increases but the pricing goes up as well.

- Term sheets are almost always nonbinding legal documents and lenders can take a lot of artistic license with how they present information. You may find a different format or wording beyond what I cover, but the same underlying concepts should be there. It is important to get to a healthy level of detail in a term sheet because all of this will flow into the definitive legal documents that follow. Better to cover a topic now, even if it involves healthy debate, than to be surprised down the road.

PREAMBLE

Every term sheet will start with a cover page(s) or a multi-paragraph narrative with niceties like, *We're a great private credit fund or venture bank. We're really excited to work with you. We have X years of experience and our team is filled with literal geniuses. Our mothers will send you a box of homemade cookies if you sign our term sheet. You should also know the other lenders you are talking to regularly kick puppies, and oh, by the way, here are some logos of the people we've financed previously.*

Maybe you won't see a list of highlights quite so graphic, but the *preamble* section tends to be a lengthy puff piece for said lender. Some of it may well be deserved, some may not, but none of it really matters. The only part that is important to note is a sentence typically at the end of the preamble or perhaps in the header or footer of the document stating, "This term sheet is for discussion purposes only and is not a legally binding contract." Essentially, a lender is saying that the numbers in the term sheet could all change meaningfully—it's a starting point, not a final agreement.

Assuming you have raised equity capital, you will perhaps remember that the term sheets you saw from VCs were also "for discussion purposes only." Nothing is a binding commitment. At the same time, if you get to the place where someone has put a full-blown term sheet in front of you, whether it's venture capital or venture debt from a bank or a private credit firm, reputation risk starts to come into play. Most lenders, whether banks or private credit, are loath to put out a term sheet with a good amount of detail and then back out. In the innovation ecosystem in particular, every company will have multiple investors on the cap table, and since the industry is so interconnected, reputation matters.

If a lender decides to bait-and-switch somebody on a particular deal, there is a cascading effect well beyond the single company who has been impacted. Every portfolio company of the various investors on the cap table is going to be aware in short order. So, while the header and footer of every term sheet is going to say, "this is not a commitment," everybody who works at a reputable firm in the venture debt landscape is going to try hard to honor the terms they've laid out. While a term sheet is not a legal document, it's also not a nothing document; it's a meaningful milestone to get a proposal because somebody's done a fair amount of work and they are trying to win your business.

BORROWER(S)

At the top of the detail portion of a term sheet, or potentially in the preamble, there is a section listing the entities who the lender is (1) providing capital to and (2) who are going to be part of the collateral pool for the new venture debt loan. If an entity is listed as a *borrower*, the lender will want to take a lien against all the assets of that entity upon execution of legal documents.

For early-stage companies that have a single Delaware (or other state) C-Corp, this is not overly complex. That one entity will be the only borrower, the lender will take a lien on all the assets of the C-Corp, the legal process will be as streamlined as it can be, and life is good.

For later-stage companies or more international start-ups, things are more complex. For example, if a company started in Canada, they might also set up a US entity early on and could have operations in both countries. Or a US-based company could have expanded quickly, with offices and people in the UK, Australia, and Singapore.

Lenders will want to understand several data points about each entity or subsidiary. Is there significant headcount in each country? Are there only expenses or expenses and revenues flowing through each country? Where will the company's IP and majority of cash balances be domiciled? In a perfect world, a lender would want to have a security interest in every entity and cover all the assets of the borrowing company. A lot of the time, though, that is not realistic or practical.

For every country involved, it takes multiple law firms to navigate the various legal environments. That adds time, expense, and a degree of uncertainty. So, most venture banks and private credit funds are willing to be pragmatic, balancing time and expense with their ability to gain a security interest in the majority of a borrower's assets. This might look like the parent company plus perhaps the most material subsidiary or a materiality threshold that could see multiple subsidiaries added to the legal agreement over time. Then, a lender would also place restrictions on how much cash could flow downstream every month to other subsidiaries and a prohibition on IP moving from the parent company without prior lender approval.

If your start-up has an entity chart that includes more than just the parent company, you want to (1) make the lender aware as early in the process as possible, (2) ensure you ask the lender to explicitly call out what entities they'd like wrapped into their security filing, and (3) have an informed perspective on how much cash needs to move regularly between those entities and consider the time and money you want to expend during the legal process that follows a term sheet. This will help you decide how much effort, if any, to put into negotiations and what entities should be included as borrowers.

COMMITMENT AMOUNT

The *commitment amount* is how much money the lender is going to make available to a company and in what currency. It's a straightforward section of the term sheet. The cleanest version is just a dollar amount that is fully available at close. You may see variations depending on the lender's comfort level providing larger commitment amounts. Sometimes, that will include performance milestone(s) to access additional tranches (fancy word for chunks or pieces) of capital. An example would be *$5M available at close with an additional $5M available upon borrower achieving $15M in trailing 12-month revenue on or before March 31, 20XX.* Lenders use milestones to ensure a company is headed in the right direction before total leverage starts to increase. This isn't necessarily a bad thing for a company, particularly if you have confidence in your plan and don't need the full amount on day one.

Other variations you might see in the commitment amount section is the entire dollar amount governed by some form of overarching borrowing formula. Such as, *$50M available at close but outstanding balance may not be greater than 1× ARR at any time.* We will cover borrowing formulas in a bit more depth later, but this is a way for a lender to have a more fluid or constant leverage test on a company. This is more common for later-stage companies with debt facilities of $30M or more.

You may also see reference to an uncommitted accordion in the commitment amount section. An accordion, in addition to being a delightful instrument, is the name lenders use for additional commitment dollars that can become available in the future but that the company does not have to pay for now. The big catch here is these dollars are "uncommitted" or "available upon review and approval," which means it is at the lender's discretion whether to make the accordion available. This is mostly marketing by a lender wanting to show they have the appetite, at least at the moment, to provide more capital to the company if needed. The amount of an uncommitted accordion will also typically not be documented in the loan agreement. Occasionally, there may be a committed accordion that is officially documented in the loan agreement. This is the version that is more valuable to a company, where access to the additional dollars is at their discretion and there is a legal commitment by the lender to provide them when requested, though that also typically includes additional fees and potentially an additional warrant as well.

USE OF PROCEEDS

The *use of proceeds* section is where lenders call out how the dollars they are providing are expected to be used. For most term sheets, this will read something like *For working capital and general corporate purposes*. Occasionally, if a venture debt facility has a specific use case, like financing an acquisition or large equipment purchase, it may be called out in this section as well. The inverse of what you see in this section, what are not allowable use cases of the money, is also worth quickly flagging. Things like secondary liquidity for founders or employees, share redemptions of any kind, or cash acquisitions are all things that would need to be explicitly approved by a lender and are not considered part of *general corporate purposes.*

LENDER(S)

Like the borrower(s) section, the *lender* part of the term sheet calls out who is going to be providing the debt capital to the company. It's possible this may sit in the preamble, but more commonly shows up in the meat of the term sheet itself. For early-stage companies involving smaller dollar amounts and mostly the venture bank market, there is typically only one lender named—the bank itself. As companies get bigger, debt facility sizes increase and private credit funds are more commonly involved. Those funds frequently use several different pools of capital.

You may see something like *Private Credit Fund III* and *Private Credit Opportunity Fund II* listed as lenders. It could also be *Venture Bank* and *Venture Bank Innovation Fund I*, if a bank has its own proprietary private credit fund (something a few of the larger banks have done).

Why does it matter who is providing the capital as long as the terms and economics work for you? Decision-making. You will want to understand who is behind each lending entity and how each party makes decisions. If the lending team you are directly working with makes decisions and speaks for both entities, great. But you may also find out that each pool of capital has different approvers in the background. That is not necessarily bad, but be sure to understand what happens if the lenders can't agree on a change you may request down the road. Almost all will have a legal document in the background dictating how disagreements between lenders are handled. Will you need to send ongoing reporting to both parties or just one? Will you need to give business updates to both lenders, or just one? All these things are good to cover up front so nobody is surprised once the deal is inked. It's not necessarily ominous or bad to have multiple lenders involved, but you want to understand who the parties are and whether one or both will need to make decisions going forward.

AVAILABILITY

If not already called out in the commitment amount section, *availability* will talk about when and how the commitment is made available. Some lenders like to be very pedantic and provide a very detailed term sheet; others may take the liberty to combine sections to shorten the document. I was frequently in the latter camp and liked shorter term sheets whenever possible. But others equate length with importance . . . ahem. You may see this section in the proposals you have in hand and it will reference what amount is available at close and what may be subject to milestones or a borrowing formula.

You will also see in this section (or the commitment amount section) if there is any required funding at close.

Required funding is a hot button for lenders, particularly private credit funds. Funds have raised money from limited partners and need to earn a healthy return for those investors in a set period. Funds try to avoid providing a venture debt commitment that subsequently goes unused. Most term sheets you will see from funds require a portion of the facility to fund at close. Something like 50% is common but they may require more than that, depending on the situation. They might also be willing to stage out when the amounts are funded. Something like 50% funded at close and another 25% required to fund within six months.

The venture bank world is less religious about requiring usage of the venture debt they provide. Don't get me wrong, they too would like to see commitments be drawn down since they will make more money. But the source of funds for venture banks, as we've discussed already, is low-cost deposits from other clients, which don't have the same return expectations or time frames attached to them.

If you are seeking a venture debt facility with optionality on whether you must draw down the money at all, it will behoove you to talk with primarily venture banks. If that is less of a concern or you plan to draw down the bulk of the funds, private credit firms are equally good parties to talk to. Required usage will be a meaningful part of negotiations that you have with lenders. They may be more willing to adjust other terms if you agree to draw down a large portion or the entirety of the commitment at close. Less so if you don't want to be required to use the debt at all. It is all a continuum.

DRAW PERIOD

If a company is not funding the full commitment amount at close, there will be a specified *draw period*. That is the time frame under which a company must use the venture debt facility, usually represented as either *XX months from close of documentation* or a specific calendar date. Draw periods tend to be longer when borrowing money from venture banks, ranging from twelve to twenty-four months. Private credit firms will want as short a draw period as possible, if any, usually less than twelve months. Companies understandably want the longest draw period possible, assuming they don't need the money immediately, because it gives them optionality on when or even whether to use the venture debt. It also allows the company to defer paying any interest expense until the debt is drawn down.

Lenders also care about the outer bound of a draw period because it is hard to know how a start-up is going to perform in the future. Everyone hopes for the best, but companies frequently take longer than expected to get traction or may never get there at all. So, lenders are trying to avoid a situation where a draw period goes out so far that the riskiness of the situation could have too wide a variance. Venture banks are willing to go longer on draw periods for companies that are overly liquid, with something like three years or more of their own cash. Even two years later, that company will still have more than a year or more of their own cash when they may ask to draw down on their venture debt facility.

All else being equal, more flexibility is generally going to be better, so I'd suggest asking for as long a draw period as you can, but every company should be aware that all draw periods come with an asterisk called a contingency funding clause. We will cover this in Chapter 7 in depth, but in short, this clause gives lenders the option not to fund some or all the commitment amount down the road. This is rarely used and, if so, mostly in situations where a company is materially underperforming and hasn't raised additional equity to rectify the issue. If you don't want to worry about that as an entrepreneur, you may want to draw down the money earlier. It will cost a bit more, but you'll sleep better at night knowing that those dollars are funded and in the company's bank account. The ability for a bank or private credit firm to claw money back after it has been funded is significantly harder than if a company has yet to borrow.

BORROWING FORMULA

If it hasn't already been covered or combined into the commitment amount or availability sections, you will likely see a specific area in a term sheet about the *borrowing formula*. For most venture debt proposals, this will simply read *None* or *N/A*. The main segment of the market for borrowing formulas is larger debt facilities ($30M+) from private credit funds. Funds want to make sure a company doesn't get over-leveraged and their proxy for that is keeping funded debt below a set ratio to revenue or ARR. The revenue or ARR multiple will move around based on the market, the investors involved, and the company's growth rate. It could range from 0.3× on the low end to greater than 1× on the high end. However, most later-stage lenders will try to keep leverage 1:1 or lower. If a company found itself outside of the borrowing formula down the road, it would need to use excess cash to pay down a portion of the venture debt to remain in compliance with the loan agreement. This can make borrowing formulas a bit of a backdoor financial covenant, because if a company doesn't have enough cash to rightsize the venture debt, they could be put into default by their lender. More on financial covenants, events of default, and what they mean in a bit.

INTEREST-ONLY PERIOD

I/O period for short, the *interest-only period* is the time frame during which a company only must pay accrued interest, not principal, each month on any borrowed dollars. That means a company can keep the loan balance static throughout the I/O period. This term tends to get a lot of attention during negotiations. Companies want this to be as long as possible, and lenders must balance the length of the I/O period against their own comfort level in delaying repayment of the debt they would like to provide to the company.

Most, if not all, I/O periods will run concurrently or in parallel with any draw period. Occasionally, you may see proposals where they run back-to-back or in serial, usually if a draw period is very short. Regardless, it is good to confirm how the I/O period works if it is not otherwise called out explicitly. For early-stage transactions, mostly from venture banks, I/O periods will normally range from twelve to twenty-four months. Interest-only periods for later-stage transactions, primarily involving private credit funds, can go out much further, sometimes as long as four to five years.

The tail end of an interest-only period tends to be one of the riskiest time frames for a lender. Their portfolio company has burned through a good chunk of the cash on the balance sheet, performance of the business may not be stellar, the outstanding principal balance of the venture debt is still static, and in a lot of cases, the company may be in the midst of—or shortly kicking off—their next equity fundraise. Which is all a way of saying that lenders would ideally like to keep interest-only periods as short as possible . . . and still win the deal.

A company is obviously in the reverse position; you want as much time as possible before you must start paying back the debt. As a middle ground, a lot of lenders are amenable to extending the I/O period if it is tied to some sort of performance milestone down the road. Something like, *Upon borrower achieving 80% of revenue plan in the next fiscal year, the I/O period will extend an additional six months.* Both parties can bring a lot of creativity to negotiations if they are motivated to get a deal done. In practice, a lot of companies also consider refinancing their existing venture debt when it gets near the end of the I/O period. Either with the same lender, assuming the company has continued making progress or raised more equity, or with other parties that are willing to provide a new facility and fresh I/O period.

AMORTIZATION PERIOD OR REPAYMENT

Yes, at some point you do, in fact, have to pay the debt or it would be called . . . equity. The *amortization period* section defines when the outstanding balance will start being paid back and over how long a period. Most venture debt structures will have a three- or four-year amortization period where the debt is paid back on a straight-line basis. Like most auto loans, the company will make equal monthly payments of outstanding principal and accrued interest until the debt is fully repaid.

Later-stage companies with larger venture debt facilities, mostly from private credit funds, may have unique repayment structures in place that could include graduated amortization where the loan is repaid in small but escalating amounts over time, such as 5% of the outstanding principal in year one, 10% in year two, 15% in year three, and the remainder due in one lump sum at the maturity date. Seen more frequently is a "bullet repayment" structure, which requires no repayment of principal until the final maturity date of the loan, when everything is due in one lump sum or "bullet."

Depending on the amount of runway a company has, it is possible that repayment of the debt may start before another equity round has been raised. That may seem counterintuitive, but most lenders want repayments to start within twenty-four months of closing. The debt will typically still be providing runway extension, but the amount of runway provided will decrease as amortization kicks in.

If possible, you want to do your best to align the draw period, interest-only period, and amortization period with the milestones that will drive your next equity raise. That may not always be attainable given what lenders think of the risk profile of your company but is worth discussing up front. Like the I/O period, lenders may be willing to lengthen repayment time frames based on hitting performance milestones, like *Upon Company achieving $XXM in trailing twelve-month revenue as*

12.31.XX, the amortization period will increase to 48 months. The amortization period is important, but I would suggest focusing most of your efforts on how long you have to draw down the money and how long the outstanding balance will stay static. Once you've raised a new round of equity, you'll likely want to change the existing venture debt structure, if not refinance the whole thing. Your lender will likely be happy to have that conversation given the recent equity validation.

MATURITY DATE

Most lenders will call out the calendar date that the proposed venture debt will be fully due or fully paid off. *Maturity date* equals drawdown period + I/O period (if not running concurrently) + amortization period. Not much to do here other than to make sure the math of the equation I just laid out is correct. Onward.

FINANCIAL COVENANTS

Covenants are things a company agrees that either it will do or it will not do for the duration of a lending relationship. There is a lengthy portion of every loan agreement devoted to affirmative (things a company must do) and negative (things a company cannot do) covenants. These can include things like requiring a company to continue to pay its taxes, keep its legal entities in good standing, not sell large portions of the business without the lender's approval, etc. One area of Covenant Land that gets particular attention during term sheet negotiations is financial covenants. These are specific financial metrics or measurements that a company must achieve or maintain; otherwise they can be put into default, and a lender can then take a variety of actions, ranging from a quick waiver to drastic actions such as sweeping cash to pay off debt.

For most venture debt transactions, particularly to earlier- and mid-stage businesses, there won't be any financial covenants. Simple.

This is driven by the recognition that in the earlier phases of a start-up's life, there is not much business to measure; the product may not even be launched yet. Even if a company has customers and early revenues, the odds the business is predictable yet are low. Lenders in the space realize that tracking any financial covenants would be hard and/or counterproductive. The other check and balance here is that there are a litany of venture banks and private credit funds vying for the business of recently funded early-stage start-ups. So even if one lender thought about adding financial covenants to their proposal, they'd immediately be out of market, so they don't bother in the first place, which is good news for start-ups. One exception that comes up in negotiations occasionally is when a company asks to significantly lower the overall economics on a proposed deal. The lender might be willing to do that but asks to add a financial covenant(s) in return. Something to consider during the give-and-take with potential lenders.

For later-stage companies with larger venture debt structures ($30M or more) that will more frequently come from private credit funds, financial covenants will be more common. Why? Later-stage businesses have more to measure and "should" be more predictable. There is also a smaller number of lenders willing to provide these large slugs of venture debt, so competitive dynamics aren't quite the same. Most often seen from the private credit funds are (1) a minimum growth requirement and (2) a minimum liquidity threshold. The growth requirement tends to be relatively light, something like requiring 5%–10% revenue growth on an ongoing basis. Minimum liquidity thresholds may require cash and accounts receivable to stay above a certain level, commonly $5M–$10M; that will allow a lender to have a larger headline number (overall commitment amount) but the amount able to extend the runway is lower. This is something you'll see in the Clearco case study coming up. Both types of covenants are meant to protect a lender from significant unexpected volatility in the underlying business. They are also designed to give the lender, company, and investors time to react before getting too close to any kind of forced sale or shutdown scenario. We talked about borrowing formulas earlier in this chapter, but you may see some sort of borrowing formula reflected as an explicit financial covenant as well.

For the subset of earlier-stage transactions that have financial covenants, you will regularly see a performance to plan requirement. Unlike a minimum growth requirement, the lender will look at a company's revenue projections and require the business to perform within 80% of that forecast, for example. Lenders might track ARR or gross margin if they are better indicators of traction in the business. The other covenant, more commonly seen among early-stage lenders, is a remaining months liquidity (RML) test. Each firm will have a slightly different definition, but they are all looking at average monthly burn and dividing that by the company's cash position. This gives an approximation of how much runway a company has left. The financial covenant will usually require the company to always have at least six—or perhaps nine—months of RML. This will limit the effective usefulness of the venture debt but, from the lender's perspective, helps avoid running the business down to zero.

Financial covenants are not the end of the world, but they are also the most common event of default in lending relationships. It is very important that the covenants are only triggered at a point where all parties agree, up front, that the business would be significantly underperforming. This also assumes you, as a borrower, have done some diligence on the lender's willingness to work with their portfolio companies when (not *if*) they end up off-plan. What happens when a company breaks a covenant? It depends. It depends on the lender's risk tolerance and the degree to which the company underperformed. In many cases where a company barely missed a covenant (84% performance to revenue plan versus an 85% requirement) a lender might quickly waive the violation or perhaps charge a small fee or just legal costs, then everyone moves on. If the underperformance is more significant, the whole structure of the deal could be up for renegotiation and the cost of the debt will likely increase in favor of the lender. In a truly dire situation, a lender could take harsh action to see its debt repaid. This happens rarely but is still something to understand well before taking venture debt from anyone.

PRO TIP: Guide Your Underwriter

A company should always guide lenders to underwrite a combination of the base and downside cases, including a decent margin or discount, when setting financial covenants. It will help avoid anyone being caught off guard when a company underperforms. More importantly, it will help ensure financial covenants only trigger when a company is significantly off-plan.

6

ECONOMIC COMPONENTS
OF THE TERM SHEET

Now that we've reviewed structural components of the term sheet, let's get into how much this will cost.

INTEREST RATE

The biggest driver of the near-term cost of a venture debt facility, the *interest rate* section of a term sheet, tends to be short. It's usually one or two lines, max. Most lenders base their interest rate on an underlying index like WSJ Prime or the secured overnight financing rate (SOFR). It would show in a proposal as *WSJ Prime + 2.00%, floating* or *SOFR + 2.00%, floating.* The word *floating* means that when the underlying index rate moves, the interest rate on the venture debt will mirror that change. Most venture debt deals done these days use floating rates. Every lender will incorporate some form of interest rate floor into their deal structure; if the underlying index moves up, the lender gets the benefit of the increase, but if rates move down, the interest rate floor holds the interest rate at the current level. An example of this would be *WSJ Prime + 2.00%, floating. Indicative Rate of X.XX%, with an interest rate floor of X.XX%.*

It is possible that a company may be able to negotiate to remove the interest rate floor. It is also possible a lender might be willing to provide the debt on a fixed interest rate basis. It really all depends on what everyone thinks about the forward interest rate curve. Lenders may be more willing to bake in some downward movement into the interest rate floor. Something like 1.00% to 2.00% below the indicative rate.

Most impactful to the overall cost of the venture debt is the margin over the underlying index. We've discussed previously, but it's worth reiterating here again that venture bank deals tend to come with lower overall economics (i.e., cost of capital to the company) given their source of funds. Since venture banks leverage their excess deposits for lending, they don't technically have a minimum of interest they need to charge for any venture debt facility. Occasionally, you might see something like *WSJ Prime – 2.00%, floating*. Why would a venture bank do this? They will likely make up for the lower interest rate with higher fees or a higher warrant that compensates for the difference, or they may just be very eager to carry the day with a new prospect.

Again, debt from private credit funds will have greater costs, with interest rates 3%–5% higher than venture bank deals. In addition to the structural differences in funding sources, their rates are higher because the quantum of the debt they provide tends to be meaningfully larger and they are taking more inherent risk with any single company. Funds also must meet the return expectations of their LPs. Private credit funds regularly have leverage on the back end of their funds, something the portfolio companies never really have to think about. It helps, in the best cases, increase the capital a private credit fund can deploy and juice their IRR. Essentially, another lender is going to look at the portfolio of loans a private credit fund has originated and give them 70%–85% of the value of those loans.

I'm telling you all this because those back-end leverage providers have specific requirements for a private credit portfolio company to be eligible to borrow against. One is that the interest rate on the loan the private credit fund has provided is not below a certain minimum threshold. Several private credit funds also pay out dividends to their LPs on a quarterly or annual basis. The cash to fund those dividends come primarily from the interest collected from borrowers. Why does this all matter? It means that private credit funds typically have their own internal interest rate floor. They aren't willing to provide capital if it doesn't have an indicative rate of XX% because they need to be able to pay regular dividends, fit the new deal into their leverage facility, or both.

One last item you may see from private credit funds is payment in kind (or PIK) interest as a potential option in a term sheet. PIK interest is a way to reduce the up-front interest expense on the debt. Any amount of PIK interest will accrue and be added to the principal balance of the outstanding debt on a monthly, quarterly, or annual basis. It will also compound over time. So, if you have a $1M loan with 4% PIK interest that accrues annually, at the end of year one, the outstanding balance would then be $1.04M. After year two, it would be $1.081M and so on. This may be worth doing if the up-front cash savings on interest expense are important to a company, but it can create a significant back-end repayment cost after several years. Buyer beware.

UP-FRONT FEES

Venture lenders are never more creative than when talking about fees. A variety of fees show up in term sheets with an even wider variety of names or titles for said fees. But they all fall into three basic categories: *up-front fees, prepayment fees,* and *back-end fees.* These categories reference the time frame each fee will be earned during the life of the lending relationship.

The most universal fee is the *up-front fee;* pretty much every firm will charge something at the beginning of a lending relationship. It may also be called a commitment fee or facility fee and it usually has some tie to the overall commitment amount. Something like *0.5% of the Commitment Amount due at close of documentation.* It may also just show up as a flat dollar amount, although typically, the lender has done a bit of simple math in the background. Up-front fees are not large economic drivers for banks since economics and deal sizes tend to be smaller. Some banks may waive their up-front fee, particularly if a company is borrowing some or all the debt at close. It can certainly be part of the negotiation. Venture bank up-front fees tend to range between 0.25% and 0.50% of a commitment amount, possibly even lower. For private credit funds, fees in general are more meaningful given the larger loan amounts involved and higher return expectations. For private credit funds, up-front fees will range between 0.50% and 2.00% of a commitment amount and are harder to negotiate in general.

PREPAYMENT FEES

The contractual life of a venture debt facility ranges from three to six years, depending on the lender and company profile. I call it "contractual" because that is what is stated in the legal documents. Every lender hopes that a new portfolio company will borrow the entire commitment amount, do great things, and the debt will stay in place until the final maturity date, hence the *prepayment fee* if it doesn't. The reality is that most venture debt loans will never get to their final maturity. Start-ups are too dynamic, in both good and bad ways. Many companies will raise more equity in eighteen to twenty-four months and will want to restructure or upsize the venture debt. Good news for most lenders. A subset of companies that raise equity will fully pay off the debt. Less good for lenders. A handful of companies may be acquired across the life of the loan and, hopefully, even a smaller number will fail or shut down. It is rare that a venture-backed company would go three years or longer without significant changes to the business.

Lenders understand those dynamics and, to one degree or another, will try to protect some of the economic upside they would have received had the venture debt stayed in place for the contractual duration. These sections in a term sheet may be called *make whole provisions, early termination fees, prepayment penalties,* or *prepayment costs.* These costs are only due if a company draws down the venture debt facility from their lender.

For venture banks, you will see less complex prepayment fee structures: likely a flat percentage of the outstanding balance when the debt is prepaid or a graduated schedule that declines over time. Something like *3% if prepaid within 12 months from close, 2% if prepaid after 12 months but prior to 24 months from close, and 1% if prepaid after 24 months.* A fair number of venture bank deals are done without prepayment fees at all. Banks are more willing to let go of these fees during the give-and-take of a broader negotiation. This is all driven by the lower return expectations banks have relative to private credit funds and the benefits they get from having a broader banking relationship with the portfolio company.

In contrast, private credit firms will always have some kind of prepayment penalty in their deal structures. Depending on the size of the transaction it is possible a prepayment fee from a fund could be a flat percentage or declining percentage over time, like venture banks. More commonly, you will see a much more "robust" make whole provision. The phrase "make whole provision" is only used by funds and means that if a loan is paid off earlier than expected, the lender wants to be "made whole" for the interest income (their revenue) they would have received otherwise. This may show up in a term sheet in a variety of ways. One version could read *Full Make Whole in Year 1, 3% Prepayment Fee in Year 2, No Prepayment Fee after 2 Years.* This means that if a company paid off the debt during the first year after closing, they would owe the outstanding principal and all future interest that would have been due. In the second year, the prepayment fee reduces to 3% of the outstanding principal balance and then no prepayment costs thereafter. The most robust version of a make whole provision would read *Borrower may prepay the loan at any time by paying the outstanding principal, accrued interest, and all future interest payments.* This may seem innocuous since the wording is relatively benign, but this means a company will pay all future interest that would have been due, regardless of when the debt is repaid. This is what is affectionately referred to in the venture-lending industry as the "full metal jacket," in that a company is not able to avoid paying all future interest that would have been due on the loan.

I have a lot of sympathy for lenders out there. It is frustrating to do a ton of work underwriting and onboarding a new portfolio company to then see that relationship end prematurely. So, most prepayment fees aren't a bad thing in and of themselves. However, entrepreneurs and companies should be sure they understand what they are signing up for with a lender. Not only does it affect the economics of the venture debt they are going to borrow, but it may also impact their flexibility down the road. For example, if you inadvertently put in place venture debt with a large make whole provision, your ability to refinance into a better deal (larger, cheaper, looser structure) from another lender down the road is also impacted, because the cost of leaving the existing provider is significant. These fees have the potential to lock you in with your current lender if you aren't careful. You need to know what you are signing up for and try to anticipate how you'd like to handle the debt over the next two to three years. If early repayment or potential restructuring is top of mind, do your best to get deal terms that allow for that without punitive fees.

Negotiate with your lender to reduce or remove the magnitude of prepayment costs as time passes. Further ask them to waive some or all the prepayment fees if you refinance or restructure the deal with the same lender. Most lenders should be willing to do that because they get the benefit of a new and, hopefully, upsized debt relationship with a company that has continued to grow. Usually a win-win for both parties.

BACK-END FEES

The last category of fees that a company will see in a venture debt term sheet is fees due at the end of the life of the loan. Unlike prepayment fees, *back-end fees* are due no matter what, assuming a company has in fact drawn down capital from their lender. You may see these called back-end fee, final payment, deferred interest, or end-of-term fee in a proposal. An example of how this will show up in the term sheet: *3% of funded amount due the earlier of final Maturity or prepayment.* Assuming the venture debt was $10M and it was all funded at close, the company would owe $300,000 at the end of the life of the loan, or sooner if repaid early. A difference to call out that you may have already noticed is that back-end fees tend to be based on funded amounts or the aggregate amount a company has drawn down on their venture debt facility. So, it doesn't matter what the outstanding principal balance is when the debt is repaid or fully paid off; what matters is how much was originally drawn down.

Lenders use back-end fees for several reasons. First, it helps to potentially lower the up-front cash interest expense for the company. If the back-end fee wasn't in the deal structure, the interest rate would likely go up. Conversely, if the back-end fee were to go up, the interest rate could potentially come down. In a lot of ways, back-end fees are like PIK interest, though importantly, the fees don't compound, making them a bit more company-friendly. Another reason lenders use a back-end fee is that it gives them a bit more control down the road when their portfolio company wants to look at refinancing the outstanding debt. If there are competitive bids from other parties, the back-end fee and prepayment fee combine to increase the cost of going with another provider. Lenders are also very aware of the average duration of an outstanding venture debt loan. By adding fees paid at the earlier of maturity or prepayment, they know a few of their loans will be repaid or refinanced earlier. When that happens, the return or IRR on that deal increases significantly.

PRO TIP: Negotiating for Cost Certainty

In my experience, fees have either been (1) a nonevent or (2) a surprise down the road that causes a lot of friction between a company, their lender, and possibly, even the board. Try to be predictive about what you will do with the outstanding debt facility after your next equity raise. Are you going to pay it off after the equity closes? Refinance it into a bigger debt structure? Keep it in place and pay it off over time? I'd suggest a willingness to trade off other economics, like a higher interest rate, to avoid the possible frustration of large fees due in the future, when you will have likely forgotten about them. Optimize for simplicity and certainty about what you are going to pay for the venture debt whenever possible. You will sleep better at night.

WARRANTS

A number of venture banks and private credit funds often describe venture debt as "non-dilutive financing." I've even been guilty of using the phrase a few times over the years. However, it is not really accurate; 90% or more of venture debt deals come with *warrants* as part of the economic package for the lender. Warrants = dilution. The correct argument a lender should make is that the all-in cost of taking on venture debt in the right situation is often five to ten times less expensive than the equivalent amount of equity dollars and subsequent dilution. Venture debt could more properly be described as "less dilutive or less expensive financing . . ." but that doesn't quite roll off the tongue, now does it? Okay, with that out of the way, let's dig into warrants.

Warrants are a right to buy company stock in the future at a set price, very much like a stock option just issued to a lender or entity, not a person. Why do lenders want to take warrants in the first place?

There is real risk in the capital they provide to innovation economy companies. This is as close to venture capital investing as any commercial lender will get. The potential equity upside from small ownership stakes in the portfolio companies that do well will help drive the overall return of the fund or the bank's loan portfolio. More critically, it will also help offset the inevitable loan losses that come if you operate in the venture-lending business long enough. Ideally, over time, the upside will outpace any losses in the portfolio.

Three major components comprise the warrant section of a term sheet. The amount of ownership or number of shares, the class of stock, and the strike price. The number of shares is the component that has the most variability in how it will show up in proposals. Some lenders will use a "coverage amount" to reflect the warrant position they'd like to take. Something like *3.00% of the Commitment Amount, vested at close.* This requires the company to do some math. Commitment Amount × 3.0% / Strike price = Number of shares. This was the way most lenders talked about a warrant two decades ago when I started my venture-lending career. I personally think it a bit silly to ask the company to do the math and it leads to confusion. The better and, thankfully, now much more common way to talk about the warrant is to state explicitly the ownership percentage a lender would like to be granted. That would read something like *Lender to be granted warrants equivalent to 0.30% of fully diluted ownership, vested at close.* This is what everyone should care about: how much ownership or dilution is being granted to the lender as part of the transaction. No extra math beyond updating the cap table. Another reason that lenders use fully diluted ownership (FDO) in the warrant section is that it protects them from additional dilution that may happen after the term sheet is signed but before the deal has officially closed. If they used a coverage amount or just stated the number of shares and a company updates their option pool or raises some additional equity before closing on the debt, the lender's ownership position would be lower than expected.

PRO TIP: Vesting Warrants Based on Usage

Most venture debt deals don't require the company to fund 100% of the debt at close. Venture banks deals commonly won't require ANY funding at close. Do your best to negotiate a staged vesting of the warrant being granted to your lender; some amount will be earned by the lender when they provide the commitment, but a portion(s) can likely be tied to when you draw down the debt. This would look something like "Lender to be granted warrants equivalent to 0.30% of fully diluted ownership; 50% of the warrant will vest at close with the remainder earned pro rata based on advances." Most lenders should be willing to have a portion of their warrant vest on usage, assuming the full amount is not expected to be funded at close.

Only two choices are available for the class of stock—common or preferred. Most lenders in today's market will ask for common stock. Why? It is rare that lenders will exercise warrants before a liquidity event so they never get any of the additional rights or protections that preferred stock would provide. With those additional rights and protections, preferred stock also comes with a higher strike price than common stock. Everything else being equal, lenders would prefer to have a lower strike price on their warrant with incrementally better upside down the road. Taking common stock also has a small side benefit in that the lender is now aligned in a good outcome with the founders and employees at their portfolio company. Occasionally, lenders will take preferred stock, usually when it has nonstandard terms like a liquidation preference greater than 1× or is participating preferred stock. A company and its board may have their own bias around the class of stock issued with the warrant as well. This will all be part of the negotiation around the overall cost or economics of the deal.

For the strike price, a lender will normally ask to use the current 409a valuation price per share when taking common stock. With preferred stock, lenders will use the strike price of the most recent preferred equity financing.

The length or duration of a warrant will vary, but ten years is the most common term. Warrants will typically allow for a cashless exercise—the lender is not required to cut a check to buy the shares when there is a liquidity event. They can simply net out the purchase price of the warrant from the upside they will get in return for their ownership position. It doesn't change the economics at all, it just streamlines the administrative overhead for everybody.

PRO TIP: Why an Entrepreneur Should Want Their Lender to Have an Ownership Stake

If a venture lender gives you a term sheet with no warrant and all the other term sheets from others include warrants, should you take that deal? Seems like a no-brainer, right? Venture debt without a warrant as part of the economics is truly "non-dilutive financing."

Well, before you sign on the dotted line, consider the following: (1) Venture lending has real risk and all lenders will lose some money over time. The only way to offset that risk is to have enough upside from the rest of the portfolio to more than make up for those losses. If a venture lender offers you a no-warrant deal, they either don't fully understand how to construct a venture-lending portfolio, don't expect to stay in the market through a full business cycle, or both. (2) Venture lenders typically have a direct piece of their compensation tied to the warrants they originate. I did at SVB and was fortunate enough to benefit from several meaningful outcomes over the years.

> For the same reason you issue stock options to employ-
> ees, having your lender and/or banker aligned in the ulti-
> mate outcome of the business pays dividends. Speaking
> from experience, I moved faster when a portfolio com-
> pany (where we had an ownership stake) needed some-
> thing unique or extra time to help with a problem they
> faced. Even when a portfolio company left SVB, I would
> still work hard if they called asking for help on anything
> because the bank and I would still benefit from the upside
> as the company continued to scale.
>
> Occasionally, private credit funds will offer later-stage
> companies no-warrant deals. Those make more sense to
> me since the company is typically de-risked significantly
> given its scale. Otherwise, consider the benefits of having
> the firm and individuals at your lender aligned and moti-
> vated to help you succeed before signing that no-warrant
> term sheet.

Financial engineering is one of the core competencies of good
lenders. Because of that, you may find a few unique terms in the warrant terms. The two most common "unique" terms are *put options*
and *penny strike price*. A put option essentially creates an economic
floor value in the warrant. With a put option, the holder is granted
the right to "put" the warrant back to the portfolio company (usually
only during M&A or IPO), which means they can force the portfolio
company to buy back the warrant at a set price, regardless of what the
shares are worth on the cap table. Lenders use put options because
it ensures that in any situation outside of complete shutdown, they
will have guaranteed upside on their warrant. Put options come into
play in my experience in two scenarios. One is when a company is in
a situation that is very risky and they only have options from one or
two lenders. Those are typically "lenders of last resort" and they are

very aware of their negotiating position. The other situation where put options come up is a bit more positive for both parties. A lender asks for 0.50% of FDO, but the company would only like to grant 0.25% of FDO. As a compromise, the lender agrees to take the lower ownership position but inserts a put option for some dollar amount, say $500K. This can be a good compromise because the lender is giving up a portion of potentially uncapped upside but is guaranteeing themselves at least some minimum return, $500K in this case, in the future. A side effect of this trade-off is that in a downside scenario, the lender will potentially be getting a meaningful return when others, preferred investors and employees, are getting close to nothing. That has the potential to get messy if not handled well.

Penny strike warrants reference a lender asking for a common stock warrant, but instead of using the current 409a valuation price per share, they ask for the price per share to be $0.01. In effect, this is like granting a lender that amount of common stock for free. If there is an outcome in the future that sees common shareholders getting any amount greater than zero, the lender will be in the money. From the company perspective, this might be a more friendly term than a put option because it doesn't mess with the order of the preference stack. It may also be another good trade-off for the lender to take a smaller ownership stake at a penny strike; the lender gives up a portion of their ownership (with potential for uncapped upside) for a more likely gain on the ownership stake they do have.

RIGHT TO INVEST

Most private credit funds and a small number of banks have raised pools of capital to invest into a subset of their portfolio companies, usually through *rights to invest* (RTIs) secured from the lending they provide. This section in a term sheet will read something like *Company shall grant to Lender the right to invest up to $1,000,000 in the next round of equity financing on the same terms, conditions, and* *pricing offered to other investors.* This is a right but not an obligation. Lenders, like investors, will want to invest in their best companies but may pass on portfolio companies that are going sideways. RTIs are different from warrants in that the company gets the benefit of the cash invested from the lender.

PRO TIP: RTI Limits

Be sure the RTI only applies to the next preferred equity financing. Occasionally, a lender may ask for an ongoing RTI in all future equity rounds beyond normal pro rata rights. This is not standard in venture lending and, more importantly, is a pain to manage. Don't do it.

GOOD FAITH DEPOSIT OR DUE DILIGENCE FEE

This section and the next one on expenses are not a part of the economic return for lenders, they are typically just passing along expenses incurred. However, these are costs that a company will bear and you should be thinking about them alongside all the other economic terms.

Every bank or private credit fund will ask for some form of *good faith deposit* (GFD). This may also be referred to as a *due diligence fee* and is the amount that will be due upon execution of the term sheet. The size will vary, but much of the time, the GFD will be the same amount as the up-front fee. Once the deposit is in hand, the lender sets it aside and starts its final approval and underwriting process alongside engaging legal counsel to draft the loan documents. If the deal closes as planned, the GFD is applied toward the combination of the up-front fee and expenses (to be defined shortly). The remaining balance, if any, is then due from the company. If the deal doesn't close for any reason other than the lender itself walking away (situation changes or lender doesn't get approval), the lender will likely keep the deposit. If there is a good reason and long-standing relationship between the investors involved and the lender, it is possible they may still be willing to refund some or all the deposit.

This is a way for banks and private credit funds to make sure they aren't left with unpaid legal fees or other expenses if a company signs their term sheet then walks away before closing. Depending on the size of the GFD, it can be a meaningful incentive not to walk away in the first place. In the scenario where the lender walks away from the transaction, they will refund the deposit in full to the company and eat any costs incurred. Look for the good faith deposit to be called out in the term sheet or in the back narrative area where you will also find the expiration date, confidentiality, and no-shop clauses. We will discuss all three of those terms in Chapter 8.

EXPENSES

Lender's *expenses* will mostly be costs that come from working with outside counsel and also include miscellaneous costs like uniform commercial code ("UCC") searches, UCC filing fees, and audit fees, but these all tend to be dwarfed by the legal costs. Like it or not, the market norm is for the company to cover the lender's expenses, like when raising venture capital.

For smaller, early-stage venture debt transactions, a lender's expenses may range from $20K to $50K. Some venture banks may be willing to pay their own legal expenses if you use shorter-form, non-negotiable documents, but often, outside counsel will be involved. For larger, later-stage transactions, a lender's expenses can be much more meaningful, ranging from $75K to $300K. Most lenders are willing to put a cap or upper limit on the expenses that need to be covered by the company, though they will always bake in margin for negotiations. They may want to put in language capping the number of turns of the legal document allowed or stating that the cap only covers reasonable levels of negotiation. Capping expenses makes sense, but as a practical matter, capping the number of turns is not very useful because it is hard to track and doesn't necessarily tie back to the overall legal costs.

Lenders have certainly been guilty of running up legal costs unnecessarily over the years, but companies and founders have been equally guilty of doing the same. This is a two-party system; both the lender and company need to focus on what is truly important, be pragmatic with most if not all issues, and keep each other's respective outside counsel focused only on areas that matter. We will touch on how to navigate a legal process efficiently in Chapter 9 with the help of two great Silicon Valley law firms that often sit on opposite sides.

CASE STUDY

A WEEK THAT WILL LIVE IN INFAMY—SVB

Until I became an author, my entire career involved working at banks. During more than twenty years at four commercial banks of varying sizes, I mostly evaluated thousands of businesses, sifting through diligence info to figure out the strengths and weaknesses of each company.

I also happen to have been an economics major, which, besides being able to draw killer graphs, means I spent my university days thinking about macroeconomic trends. Normal classroom discussions were on topics like interest rate policy and its effect on monetary policy, government bonds, and the overall economy. So, it pains me to say that I was mostly oblivious to the issues my employer, SVB, was facing at the tail end of 2022. There were a few rumblings internally about SVB's bond portfolio having issues in December of that year, but the first time I really became aware of the scale of the potential problem came from Twitter:

Raging Capital Ventures ✓
@RagingVentures · Follow

Silicon Valley Bank $SIVB reports earnings tomorrow

Investors have rightfully been fixated on $SIVB's large exposure to the stressed venture world, with the stock down a lot.

However, dig just a little deeper, and you will find a much bigger set of problems at $SIVB... 1/10

11:38 AM · Jan 18, 2023

♥ 5.5K   💬 Reply   ⊘ Copy link

Read 163 replies

In the January 2023 thread, Raging Capital Ventures' founder Bill Martin correctly put a spotlight on SVB's bond portfolio. The bank had more than $90B of held-to-maturity (HTM) bonds in late 2022. Remember, banks invest excess deposits that they can't lend out into securities like government bonds. That year, the Federal Reserve (Fed) began increasing interest rates rapidly. From March 2022 to December 2022, the federal funds rate increased by 400bps, or 4%, the fastest increase in interest rates over a one-year period in the Fed's modern history.

A quick reminder: The face value of a bond moves in the opposite direction of interest rates. Say you bought a $100 bond that pays 3% per year for ten years. The following year, interest rates move up to 5%. Your $100 bond, now paying less interest than newly issued bonds, is worth less, call it $92, assuming you sell before the ten-year maturity date. If you don't sell, you can keep collecting 3% interest per year and get your $100 back at the end of year ten.

In that situation, the difference between what you paid for your bond and the current face value of the bond is an *unrealized loss*. An $8 unrealized loss, to be precise. If the bond is held to maturity, the loss never becomes "realized"—a nice accounting term used to acknowledge the now-lower market value of the bond but that has no immediate monetary impact. However, if you sell the bond before maturity, the loss becomes very real.

Bill Martin's thread highlighted the magnitude of the same problem for SVB. The $90B of HTM securities carried an unrealized loss of $16B exiting 2022, compared to SVB's equity base at the same time of $11.5B. Effectively, that meant if the bank needed to liquidate the full HTM portfolio, it would be out of business. The operative word in the last sentence is "needed." At the time of Bill's commentary, the concern was theoretical because SVB had more than $175B of deposits and another $170B of funds managed for clients in off-balance sheet investments.

The executive leadership of the bank and most employees, including me, thought the institution had ample cushion to solve the issue within the HTM securities portfolio. Options included enticing some off-balance sheet funds to move back into regular deposit accounts, slowing loan origination to avoid using excess deposits, or selling a portion of the bond portfolio at a loss while also raising equity. In short, most SVBers (SVB employees) did not think the bank would "need" to sell the entirety of its HTM portfolio or face anything like an existential crisis.

I joined SVB in the depths of the Global Financial Crisis in early 2009. Hundreds of banks were failing, and the stock market was in a state of panic. My first three months on the job included several all-employee calls to announce that the bank (1) would take a large chunk of TARP money from the government, (2) there would be no salary increases that year for anyone, and (3) there would be no year-end bonuses paid for the prior year's work. In March 2009, SVB stock hit a ten-year low of $11 per share. I did my best to assure my new colleagues that the timing of those announcements—the stock price low point and my joining the bank—were purely coincidental.

Looking back, I wish we could have known that the market had just hit bottom and that the innovation economy was starting what would become a generational fifteen-year bull market run. SVB was the only publicly traded bank that was solely focused on the innovation economy. That insulated the institution from the broader mortgage crisis that was affecting other banks and put SVB in a position to benefit from the zero-interest rate policy that the Fed started pursuing in 2009 and continued for most of the next decade.

The scale of growth at SVB over the following twelve years was truly unprecedented in the banking industry. Total client funds, the combination of on-balance sheet deposits plus off-balance sheet client investments, grew from $25B in 2009 to $375B in late 2021, a 14× increase. Total loans grew from $4.5B in 2009 to $74B in late 2021, more than a 15× increase. SVB's stock price hit an all-time intraday high of

$763 per share in mid-November 2021, a staggering 68× increase from the March 2009 low.

The bank worked with over 50% of the venture-backed companies in the United States at its high point. Over two-thirds of the active venture capital funds were bank clients. Across the 2010s, SVB launched or expanded offices in China, the UK, Ireland, Germany, Sweden, and Canada. We also expanded into different business linesin 2018 acquiring Leerink Partners, which became the basis for the investment banking arm of SVB, SVB Securities. WestRiver Group was acquired in 2020 to further expand the bank's growing off-balance sheet private credit fund capabilities.

SVB's growth mirrored that of the broader innovation economy, which was on even more of a generational run. Annual venture capital investment in the US went from a low of $25B in 2010 to $50B in 2015, exceeding the last high point in the dot-com boom, and continued its torrid growth to more than $350B in 2021. New venture-backed company formation more than tripled across the same time period, to over 6,000 companies annually in 2021.

To be a part of SVB during this rocket ship ride was the job of a lifetime. The financial performance of the bank was amazing on its own, but the culture and caliber of the people we worked with every day was what really made the experience so rewarding.

SVB didn't feel like a bank; it was not old nor stodgy. Serving the innovation economy meant we had to be dynamic—adding new products when the industry needed them, frequently updating policy to adapt to new market dynamics, and being willing to suspend disbelief when hearing an entrepreneur's crazy new business idea. I was attracted to SVB specifically because it didn't feel like the three banks I had worked at previously.

That entrepreneurial culture was part of the allure, but the caliber of the people also matched it. Skill set mattered, but who you were as a person mattered more; we screened for "good humans" first and skill set second. I use that phrase "good humans" intentionally. It meant you led with empathy, could work well with a team, built excellent relationships, took ownership, and cared about the overall business. It meant that we hired people from a variety of backgrounds, not just finance people. English majors, history majors, and former members of the military were a handful of the disparate backgrounds you might find in the organization.

As much as I hate to say it, the technical skills involved in venture-lending are not rocket science. With excellent teachers and mentors to learn from, anyone with a decent IQ could pick it up. However, the soft skills, including intellectual curiosity, empathy, communication (spoken and written), and competitive drive were much harder to teach.

Besides making SVB a great place to work, the focus on screening for "good humans" when hiring was a key component of the business model. One of the bank's core strengths was relationship-building with the hope of working with entrepreneurs and investors across their careers. This meant employees needed to thrive in building long-term multi-turn relationships. SVB also needed employees who would care about and work for each other. Why?

I might talk with an investor who shared a critical piece of information about her firm or another portfolio company, neither of which I worked with directly, but that would meaningfully impact another person or team at SVB. A lot of times, that tidbit of info could be the difference between winning new banking business, a competitive venture debt process, or anticipating issues with a portfolio company. I had to be intrinsically motivated to understand the importance of that information and take time out of my day to share it with others. Saying it is easy but doing it is hard.

SVB was filled with people who thrived on helping each other. Some of my closest friends to this day are current and former SVBers. It was truly a unique place to work. If you ask any current or former

SVB employee what it is like, you will likely hear a version of what I just described. Perhaps we should have considered starting a cult; we were that good at indoctrinating people.

By mid-2022, the innovation economy was coming down from its high point and bifurcating into AI and everything else. The low-interest-rate environment was no more and the COVID tech bump had run its course. Deposit inflows at SVB slowed and companies cared more about the yield on the deposit dollars they had. The net effect was that SVB's on-balance sheet deposits started to decline and more of the remaining dollars were moved into interest-bearing accounts instead of just checking accounts.

The shift in deposit mix increased SVB's cost of funds, reducing interest margin (interest on a loan minus cost of funds) and overall profitability. For the first time in more than a decade, the bank was starting to rein in expenses to address the issue. At this time, I was Head of Credit Solutions for SVB Canada and effectively the country's number two executive reporting to the Head of Canada. We were also the fastest-growing market across SVB—partly because our team was outstanding and partly because we were starting from a small base.

Even in our fast-growing market, the Head of Canada and I were asked to game plan a 5% to 10% reduction in headcount. Other parts of the bank were facing similar or higher headcount reduction targets. No decisions had been made, but those recommendations would likely have been implemented in Q2 2023.

Even with the deteriorating financial outlook, looming layoffs, and Bill Martin's Twitter thread, most of us SVBers still didn't have bank failure on our bingo card. In our minds, it was natural that after such a long market upswing there would be a subsequent belt-tightening. Our lending portfolio was also well positioned to weather a downturn—as we had over multiple previous business cycles. Less than 5% of the portfolio was early-stage venture debt, the riskiest type of lending SVB provided, and there were ample loan loss reserves set aside.

SVB was a central cog in the innovation ecosystem and we all believed that would continue. You can go back and read the Q4 2022 earnings release and presentation at ir.svb.com. It is a time capsule into SVB's thinking just months before failure with almost no signs of the impending crisis.

That (over)confidence made the internal announcement by SVB CEO Greg Becker on Wednesday, March 8, 2023, so jarring. Greg announced the bank had sold its entire $21B of available for sale (AFS) bond portfolio at a $1.8B loss (AFS bonds was the other type of fixed income instrument the bank was holding). After the AFS sale, the only bonds left would be the HTM portfolio. To offset the impact of the loss causes by the AFS sale, SVB was raising more than $2B of equity in a variety of forms. Key word, "raising." The new equity had not yet closed as of Wednesday afternoon, with two more trading days before the potential respite of the weekend. Besides informing employees, a press release publicly distributed the same information after the financial markets had closed.

The announcement became a very public confirmation that SVB was facing the exact existential issue raised by Bill Martin in early January. To say it spooked the market and the tech ecosystem would be a gross understatement. Twitter was awash with commentary about the precarious position SVB was in. WhatsApp groups with entrepreneurs and investors were equally on fire; most were telling companies and venture funds to move their money out of the bank ASAP. Some of those private discussions had started days and even weeks earlier by folks who were clearly better than me at spotting potential bank failure.

On Thursday, March 9, SVB's stock price opened at $176 per share, an overnight drop of 34%. Our CEO and several other senior executives were doing conference calls with investors and portfolio companies to stave off panic. The feedback from attendees of those calls was . . . not reassuring. Every outward-facing SVBer was fielding calls with portfolio companies and individual investors to reassure them.

112 · VENTURE DEBT DEALS

That was the case at SVB Canada; our team talked with every single portfolio company that day.

SVB Canada was only a lending branch, which meant most of our portfolio companies did not have deposits at risk, so they were not quite as spooked as US-based companies. I was keeping tabs on colleagues across the US organization and things did not sound good. Companies and investors were scrambling to open new bank accounts elsewhere and quickly transfer their money out. As the markets closed Thursday afternoon, the stock was down another 40% to $106 per share.

For years, SVB sent a daily email detailing any money movement into or out of the bank and was a useful tool for keeping tabs on significant transfers within one's portfolio and across the broader bank. It was automatically sent at 3:30 p.m. Pacific Time each weekday.

Even though I was in a full-time role with SVB Canada, I was only in the country one week per month as a result of starting the role during COVID. I was in Toronto the week this was all happening. My credit solutions team and I were sharing a few bottles of wine on Thursday evening in our office lounge to help us process the magnitude of what was going on.

We were taking guesses about how much money had left the bank that day. I think the highest number around the table was $10B. At 6:30 p.m. ET, the daily money movement email hit our inboxes. More than $40B had left the bank that day. A staggering amount. We drank the last of our wine and headed home, not knowing what the next day would bring.

In my case, I was up early the next morning, March 10. Sleep was hard to come by and I was also flying home to San Francisco. The morning direct flight from Pearson Airport left at 6:10 a.m. ET, early enough already, and made worse by still being partly on West Coast time. Customs was easy since I had NEXUS, so there was time to kill before boarding. The headlines were not reassuring.

Many were speculating when—not if—the FDIC would step in to take over SVB.

As I boarded the plane, I hoped the bank might at least survive until the weekend; perhaps it would raise equity or borrow from the Fed's discount window. I wasn't optimistic but was holding on to the possibility that my employer might survive. The head flight attendant gave the normal welcome aboard and overhead bag guidance. He finished by letting everyone know the plane would not have Wi-Fi as planned.

My fellow passengers groaned at the news but I was relieved that I would have six hours of "calm" before getting back online in San Francisco. The flight was a blur; I honestly can't remember what I spent the time doing. We landed on what was a sunny late winter day, and when I turned on my phone, I received a deluge of text messages from colleagues, friends, and family, which I ignored (sorry, Mom). Instead, I opened the *Wall Street Journal* on my phone. The lead story was "Silicon Valley Bank Closed by Regulators, FDIC Takes Over." My employer of fourteen years had become the third-largest bank failure in US history.

AFTERMATH

The FDIC takeover on Friday, March 10, 2023, was far from the end of the panic running rampant in the innovation ecosystem. A significant number of portfolio companies and venture funds at the bank had deposits well over the $250K FDIC insurance limit. Usually, the FDIC did not backstop balances above those limits.

The timing of the takeover didn't help things either. The twelfth or thirteenth of any month is when mid-month payroll debits hit. If funds were unavailable the following Monday, paychecks for hundreds of thousands of start-up employees were in jeopardy, on top of the thousands of companies that would fail shortly thereafter.

Politics was also impeding sound decision-making. Neither party in Washington wanted to be seen bailing out well-heeled venture capitalists and start-ups that had raised tens of millions of dollars. A lot of the early voices opining on SVB's failure advocated letting the investors and start-up companies take the hit. It is rare to see Democrats and Republicans agree on anything these days, but in the early hours after SVB's failure, they were on the same side for once.

If you were in the industry when SVB failed, you remember the stress of that weekend. Entrepreneurs and companies did everything they could to get new bank accounts opened at other institutions. Investors scrambled to help fund their portfolio companies with new equity or lines of credit where possible. Lawyers across Silicon Valley slept in their offices, working nonstop to properly document these moves. SVBers fielded calls the entire weekend from people desperate for any new information. We were also unsure whether we even had jobs anymore. It was a truly surreal experience.

Thankfully, cooler heads in government prevailed after intense lobbying from start-ups, investors, and other like-minded groups; the systemic risk of letting the lion's share of SVB's deposits go away was too great. The FDIC announced late on Sunday, March 12, that it would make every depositor of the bank whole. SVB would also be open for business the next day as usual, now as a bridge bank, fully controlled by the FDIC. The sense of relief in the innovation ecosystem was palpable.

SVB was toppled in the end by making a basic banking error: Executive leadership did not anticipate or hedge against the potential for significant interest rate movement, leaving the organization susceptible to a good old-fashioned bank run. Everything else downstream (misinformation, investors publicly encouraging the bank run, etc.) of the interest rate decision was noise. For years, SVBers counseled portfolio companies of all types never to risk principal or liquidity with the venture capital dollars they raised in pursuit of higher yield. I've said that line verbatim hundreds of times over my career when a founder asked about potential investment options after an equity raise. Ironic that the bank didn't heed the same prescient advice.

From where I sit, I don't think there was anything criminal or immoral involved, just a handful of misguided business decisions that killed the institution where I thought I'd spend the rest of my career. I was filled with a combination of sadness and anger. Dwarfing my emotions was the immense financial impact the failure had on SVB stockholders (including a large number of employees) who lost everything. Deferred compensation participants (current and already retired SVBers) ultimately lost more than half of what they had set aside for retirement because of the bank's failure. And the innovation economy worldwide went through enormous turmoil, then lost one of its most central players and advocates.

I continue to be proud of what SVB built and I still mourn the loss several years later; I think most current and former SVBers feel similarly. It was truly a unique and lovely place to work. I will now step off my "I heart SVB" soapbox to regale you with the details of the formal unwinding of my former employer.

SVB Financial Group, or SVBFG, was the bank holding company and publicly traded entity that SVB shareholders owned. The biggest component of SVBFG was Silicon Valley Bank that the FDIC seized on March 10. SVB Canada was taken over by OSFI on March 12 (more on that situation in the upcoming Clearco case study). SVB UK was taken over by the Bank of England and sold for one pound to HSBC on March 13. BaFin, the regulatory body in Germany, imposed a moratorium on SVB Germany on March 13 that was later put into insolvency proceedings. SSVB, the bank's joint venture in China with Shanghai Pudong Development Bank (SPDB), was allowed to continue to operate by Chinese regulators and ultimately subsumed as a wholly owned subsidiary of SPDB in August 2024. There is an excellent book on SVB's Chinese operation, *The China Business Conundrum*, recently published by Ken Wilcox, former CEO (not during the failure) of SVB. It details the events leading up to SVB's failure and is worth a read.

SVBFG filed for bankruptcy on March 15 and started to sell any assets it had left. After two weeks in bridge bank purgatory, Silicon

Valley Bank US was purchased by First Citizens Bank. SVB Securities, part of SVBFG, was purchased in July 2023 with a management buy-out led by Jeff Leerink, head of SVB Securities and founder of Leerink Partners. In March 2024, the Indian subsidiary (SVB Global Services India) was also sold to First Citizens Bank. Most recently, in May 2024, SVB Capital was sold to Pinegrove Capital Partners. Several years on, a few assets still sit within SVBFG (now out of bankruptcy) and will slowly be monetized over time.

KEY TAKEAWAYS

SVB continues as part of First Citizens Bank. Purchased in March 2023, the organization has carried on supporting the innovation economy in the US as a division within FCB. The international footprint is gone, but the firm is still a very prominent player in banking and lending to start-ups and venture funds. Many of the good humans I referenced earlier have continued there as part of the larger, combined bank.

Venture debt was not the cause of SVB's failure. Ironically, the thing that was perceived as the "risky" part of SVB's business, venture debt, was not the cause of the bank's demise. Far from it. SVB's venture debt portfolio generated north of $1B in upside (warrant gains minus venture debt loan losses) over the twenty years preceding the failure; the institution was well positioned to navigate the slowing pace of venture investment.

Evidence of the quality of the loan portfolio and the underlying business model came when First Citizens Bank acquired SVB's US banking operation. They kept Marc Cadieux—SVB's chief credit officer and a thirty-year veteran of the bank—promoting him to run the entire SVB commercial division. They also told the broader SVB team, "We want you back doing what made SVB so unique, including lending money [venture debt] to innovation economy companies."

The number of credible players in venture lending increased meaningfully after SVB's failure. During SVB's two weeks in limbo as a bridge bank (owned and operated by the FDIC), a group of talented SVBers left to join Stifel's commercial bank to bolster its existing venture banking practice. Two weeks after SVB was acquired, another group of SVBers left to start a US tech practice at HSBC, adding to SVB's former UK operation that was now controlled by HSBC. A third group of SVBers left in Q2 2023 to expand the existing tech banking practice at MUFG. Other banks and private credit funds in the US hired SVBers in ones and twos as the dust settled from the failure and FCB's acquisition.

Among my former colleagues at SVB Canada, a handful of folks joined the acquirer of the Canadian loan portfolio, National Bank. Another group joined RBCx, forming a new Life Science & Healthcare practice. A third group left to build a brand-new innovation banking practice at TD. The rest split out among private equity, private credit, and different industries entirely.

All told, there are several new, well-resourced innovation banking practices in North America and an even larger number of players who have leveled up their teams, on top of SVB being back in business as part of FCB.

It is a good time to be in the market for venture debt. All the newly formed innovation banking practices are vying for market share in a variety of ways, but in particular, by being very aggressive when lending. SVB wants to continue showing that it is still a very active player in the ecosystem, so it too has been aggressive with its venture lending efforts.

On top of the expansion of the innovation banking landscape, private credit fund participation in the tech ecosystem has never been greater. This was partly driven by the desire to win market share as SVB navigated failure and then acquisition. Another was the increasing size of the average debt needed by later-stage companies. As borrowing needs for a business reached $75M or greater, more private credit funds felt the effort to pursue these types of companies was finally worth it.

All of this means that any start-up will have more potential lending partners to choose from than ever before. In what will be only the second or third time, I will have leveraged my economics degree... competition in a market is a good thing.

Keeping all your cash at one bank is no more. Historically, when venture banks lent money to a company, they required the business to keep all its deposits at the bank. This requirement served several purposes. First, it gave banks a cheap source of funding for lending products. Second, it contributed to the overall economic return of each venture debt transaction. Third, it increased the lifetime value of each transaction because of the inherent friction, or general lack of fun, when moving bank accounts. Once a company transitioned its banking, the odds it moved again were low. Last, the deposit requirement was good risk management as it allowed RMs and PMs to see all cash in real time. That kind of visibility is very useful when a venture-backed start-up is going through an equity fundraise.

For years, nobody blinked an eye at the requirement. That all changed after SVB's failure. Entrepreneurs, finance teams, and boards are very aware of the risk that comes with keeping all of their capital on the balance sheet of one bank. Every company now has at least two banking relationships; most have a primary bank to hold the bulk of their cash and a backup bank just in case, solving one of the big choke points that happened the weekend of SVB's failure—actually getting new accounts open.

Most companies now keep no more than a few months of payroll in a primary bank's checking account, usually less than $1M. The bulk of their cash sits in off-balance sheet funds that are invested in government treasuries, agencies, or insured cash-sweep (ICS). ICS has been around for years, but it really took off in the tech ecosystem after SVB's failure. I suspect multiple banking relationships and keeping funds from being concentrated on a single bank's balance sheet are here to stay.

7

CONTROL COMPONENTS
OF THE TERM SHEET

Several sections in a term sheet give brief overviews of what will end up becoming large parts of the definitive loan agreement. These areas tend to be about controls a lender wants to have over the new portfolio company. Like, defining what a company can do in the ordinary course of business, what it cannot do during the lending relationship, and what actions the company might take that will put it offside or in default with its lender.

I've spent countless hours on these sections during term sheet back-and-forth, with even more time spent in negotiating the much longer loan agreements. Even with all that experience, I am not close to being a lawyer, nor do I play one on TV. I thought it prudent to bring in a few experts who work day in and day out negotiating definitive loan agreements on behalf of lenders AND portfolio companies.

Laurie Hutchins is a partner at DLA Piper and the head of their venture-lending practice. DLA Piper is one of the top law firms representing lenders (banks and private credit funds) across the world. During my time at SVB, we worked with DLA Piper extensively. Laurie and I worked together on a variety of venture debt transactions with some great portfolio companies over the years.

Sam Angus and Eric Shedlosky are both partners at Fenwick & West ("Fenwick"). Sam has spent more than three decades representing venture-backed companies of all types and sizes. He was on the other side of the table from me during the Airbnb transaction, one of my case studies. Eric specializes in navigating debt and corporate finance transactions for the broader Fenwick partnership and their portfolio companies. Fenwick has been a stalwart in Silicon Valley and the innovation economy for more than fifty years.

Laurie, Sam, and Eric were kind enough to overlook my playful comments about lawyers earlier in the book and sat down with me to discuss venture debt term sheets and the underlying loan documents that regularly become flashpoints during negotiation. They also outlined some best practices on how to run an efficient venture debt fundraise. You'll find thoughts from them sprinkled throughout this chapter and Chapter 9 in text boxes titled either *The Company Legal Perspective* (Fenwick's commentary) or *The Lender Legal Perspective* (DLA Piper's commentary). Apologies in advance since they are all smarter than me and use a lot of multi-syllabic words. Please enjoy the pro bono legal advice.

REPORTING REQUIREMENTS

Every lender will ask for some sort of ongoing reporting from their portfolio company for the duration of their relationship; it is the primary way a venture bank or private credit fund monitors the performance of the company. Reporting requirements are also a very basic ongoing confirmation that the company has some amount of accounting and governance processes in place. Most venture lenders will ask for the same reports on similar intervals with a few differences around the edges.

Monthly company-prepared financials are something every lender will want. This includes the balance sheet, income statement, and frequently, a cash flow statement. Depending on the lender, this may also include accounts receivable (A/R) and accounts payable (A/P) aging reports. Some lenders will require a monthly compliance certificate that needs to be executed by a signatory to the original loan documents. A compliance certificate is a short document that affirms the company is submitting the financials and attesting that they are accurate to the best of their knowledge. The compliance certificate reaffirms that the company continues to be in compliance with all the other covenants in the loan agreement. If financial covenants are part of the deal structure, a compliance certificate will list each covenant and the company will attest whether they are in compliance. The monthly company-prepared financials, agings, and compliance certificate will usually be due to the lender within thirty days of month-end.

All private credit funds and a decent number of venture banks will require board materials to be sent over within ten days of each board meeting. Some companies may be hesitant to share full board decks with their lender given the depth and potential sensitivity of the information they contain. Most lenders are willing to let a company redact or remove anything they deem overly sensitive, a conflict of interest, or a risk to attorney-client privilege, such as employee HR matters, acquisition discussions, etc. Receiving board materials on a regular basis will help lenders ask more relevant questions during ongoing catch-ups with a portfolio company. Even better, it may negate the need to have meetings as often because the lender can already read about what is and is not working in the deck.

On an annual basis, every lender will want to see company-prepared year-end financials within thirty days of year-end. They also frequently require audited annual financials to be delivered within 180 days of year-end. It used to be common for start-ups not to bother doing audits until they were a year or two out from going public, but today, audited financials are more frequently requested, even for early-stage companies. Venture investors would never be accused of always choosing good governance over speed, but audits seem to be one area where they have increasingly held the line. Lenders will either require the audited financials outright or, if a company is very early-stage, they will ask for audited financials only if required by the board. For a later-stage company, lenders may also require the auditing work be done by a "nationally recognized" firm.

Annual updated forecasts will be due to lenders within thirty days of board approval and usually on or before the end of a company's fiscal Q1. There is also generally a catch-all requirement that if a company "officially" updates its forecast throughout any given year, the lender would need to see a copy of that forecast within thirty days.

Two other reporting items may be individually called out in this section but don't have a set time frame. Whenever a company makes meaningful revisions to its cap table outside of things like employee option grants, lenders will want to see the updated version. Along similar lines, whenever a company completes an updated 409a valuation, lenders will want to see a copy. If a company moves toward annual 409a valuation updates, more common for later-stage businesses, this will become an annual requirement.

Beyond documents or reports that are specifically mentioned, lenders have a catch-all such as *Other financial information as reasonably requested by Lender.* This lets them ask for items in the future that they don't call out specifically at the start. You may also see a requirement to send your lender any documents that are regularly shared with other preferred stock shareholders. Private credit funds will use this occasionally as their version of a catch-all statement.

What is a lender doing in the background when they receive reporting from a portfolio company? I mentioned already that they are monitoring the performance and overall health of the company, but let's unpack what that means. When a company sends over its monthly financials, a lender is typically checking the performance relative to the most recent forecast they have, particularly the income statement. Are revenue, margins, OPEX and burn tracking to plan? All venture banks and private credit funds maintain an ongoing view of the risk of any portfolio company, called a *risk rating*, that is based on a variety of qualitative and quantitative factors. The two biggest quantitative factors that drive risk rating decisions are performance to plan and months of runway remaining.

Lenders have varying internal thresholds related to performance to plan. If a company is more than 20% off its revenue forecast, for example, a lender may need to downgrade the risk rating for the company. If the company is more than 50% off its revenue forecast, a lender will need to downgrade its risk rating more substantially and will likely increase monitoring with more frequent meetings with the company and its investors. With updated monthly financials in hand, lenders will quickly do the math on months of runway remaining, which may offset or increase any performance to plan concerns. Companies with more than eighteen months of runway, particularly if the debt hasn't been fully drawn down, won't be as concerning to most lenders. A lot can change in that time frame at the company itself and in the broader market (capital markets, valuation multiples, etc.), so it's a problem for another day. It is a different story for companies that are approaching or below twelve months of runway, particularly if all the debt has been drawn down; the current performance of the business is what is likely to drive new equity investor interest or the lack thereof. Even if performance is good, as runway drops below twelve months, lenders will downgrade their internal risk rating and want to keep close tabs on the ongoing equity fundraise.

BANKING REQUIREMENTS

We covered the underlying business models of venture banks and private credit funds earlier in the book and nowhere are those differences more apparent than in the *banking requirements* part of a term sheet. For private credit funds, this section is simple since they are agnostic to where a company does its banking. If the company has all their money at one institution, great. If they have it split across five institutions (to illustrate the point; please don't do this), that's fine too.

The only thing a private credit fund will care about is perfecting their security interest in the company's funds, wherever they reside. That means that while a company working with a private credit fund won't be forced to move money to a new bank when the transaction closes, they will be required to set up a *deposit account control agreement* (DACA) for every banking relationship they do have. DACAs are fun little documents that tell a bank that their customer/company has a lending relationship in place with a third party, the private credit fund in this case.

Once in place, a DACA allows that private credit fund to perfect its security interest in the bank account and take control of those bank accounts in the future if the portfolio company is in default (more to come on that) and the lender has decided to act. Taking over the bank accounts of an underlying portfolio company is a drastic step, usually used as a last resort, in cases of fraud or imminent company failure. Assuming you've chosen the right lending partner, this shouldn't be much of a concern.

Every bank tends to have their own form of DACA. I highly recommend you use the form each bank provides, as is. Don't try to negotiate the form, even if your law firm thinks it is worthwhile (sorry, Laurie, Sam, and Eric). I promise it is not worthwhile. Negotiating the DACA form will drag out the closing process, cost more money in legal fees than the effort is worth, and increase the number of gray hairs on everyone's head.

Venture banks will have different language in the banking requirements section of a term sheet. It will commonly read something like *Company to maintain 80% of deposit account balances and primary operating accounts at Bank. Excess cash above $500,000 in aggregate outside Bank or Bank's Affiliates will be subject to Deposit Account Control Agreement.* Why the difference? Innovation banks hope to make a good return on the venture debt itself, but a key driver for why they provide the capital (with lower cost than private credit, in most cases) is to acquire the broader banking relationship, which they hope to maintain well beyond the life of the venture debt. So, if you are banking somewhere else and decide to move forward with another venture bank term sheet, you'll need to plan on moving your banking during the closing process. Good news is that most venture banks will give a new portfolio company 90–120 days to fully transition their banking over, if needed. The other good news is that a DACA isn't required for the balances held at the bank that is providing the venture debt.

In the immediate aftermath of SVB's failure (and subsequent acquisition/resurgence), all the venture banks dropped the required cash number to as low as 50%. Since 2023, the banking requirement levels have slowly increased back up to 70%–80%. Venture banks will allow portfolio companies to maintain backup banking relationships elsewhere; they just want to limit how much cash sits at those institutions. This addresses one of the biggest choke points during the two days of madness that was SVB's collapse—opening new bank accounts at other institutions.

Innovation banks may be willing to allow for less than 70% of cash held at their bank as part of their deal structure if the company has a sizable international footprint or expects to expand to other countries in the near term. Usually, global operations are a sign that a company is scaling (a good thing), and lenders will not want to prohibit operating cash needs that are in the normal course of business. However, a bank or private credit fund may still want to limit how much cash sits internationally at any given time and may restrict how much cash can be sent to or kept at international subsidiaries on a monthly or annual basis.

PRO TIP: Off-Balance Sheet Options

If you do take capital from a venture bank and have some form of banking requirement as part of the deal structure, confirm that the bank has solid off-balance sheet investment options and that those balances count toward the banking requirement percentage. The other issue that SVB's failure exposed was the amount of money held in operating accounts well over FDIC limits; everything over $250K was potentially at risk.

Most banks have off-balance sheet options available—liquid money market funds with underlying investments in US treasuries and agencies. These take a variety of forms. One of the more common products used is called insured cash sweep (ICS) that sets a peg balance ($250K, for example) then spreads the amount over the peg balance across a variety of banks so that all the funds are covered by FDIC insurance. Before signing the term sheet, ensure your bank's off-balance sheet options and confirm that any amount held there also counts toward the total banking relationship percentage.

One other area that has become a point of negotiation is a company's corporate credit card program. The rise of fintechs, such as Brex and Ramp, which provide corporate card programs have materially affected what was historically a large source of revenue for venture banks. Some banks allow preexisting credit card programs with fintechs to stay in place. Some banks do not and want those programs transitioned to the bank's own offerings. Be cognizant of the switching costs even if it's just the time involved. Also know that if a venture bank doesn't get the benefit of a corporate card relationship, their willingness to change other parts of their venture debt deal structure or pricing may be lower. All these deal points are interrelated.

EVENTS OF DEFAULT

This is arguably the section of a term sheet that contains the smallest amount of detail relative to how much of the legal documents will be spent covering these topics. In a term sheet, you may see this section called *events of default, other conditions, contract terms* or it may end up just being a paragraph in the narrative at the end of the document. The language is meant to be a very brief summary of the range of terms and conditions including affirmative and negative covenants, permitted acquisitions and investments, and events of default that will be fully flushed out in the legal documents, after the term sheet is executed.

Two specific terms, *financial covenants* and *material adverse change* (MAC) *clauses*, are commonly split out from events of default into their own sections in the term sheet given the amount of focus and negotiation they both receive. We've already discussed financial covenants, and we will cover the MAC clause in the next section, but both would fall into discussions about events of default as well.

Some examples of language you'd see in the events of default section include *Loan documentation will include standard Events of Default customary for this type of facility, including Material Adverse Change language* or *Within the loan agreement there will be restrictions on activities customary for similar transactions of this type including, without limitation, restrictions on liens and indebtedness, payment of cash dividends, asset dispositions and down streaming, guaranties, mergers, etc.*

Assuming a company has good outside counsel helping to navigate the venture debt process, this section won't be much of a concern. A lot of negotiations can be tabled until you are past the term sheet and working through the legal process. All lenders expect give-and-take on these areas in the legal documents; it rarely becomes something that kills a transaction. If there is a particular thing a company does in the ordinary course of business or expects to need significant flexibility from a lender in the legal documents, it may be worth discussing that during the term sheet phase. That is the point where companies will have the most negotiating leverage, but it also allows a lender to evaluate what added risk might be involved. Examples of things that may be worth bringing up at the term sheet stage include: (1) if a company wants to be allowed to take on large amount of specific vendor financing alongside the venture debt to help finance servers or other hard assets, (2) if the company expects to make a sizable acquisition in the next six to twelve months and would like get approval now, or (3) if the company has an international subsidiary that will need significant investment over the next twelve to eighteen months.

Regardless of what language ends up being used in events of default and in the broader legal documents, what happens when a company is in default? Good question. The real answer is . . . it depends. First, what is the degree or magnitude of the default? Second, what is the lending philosophy, reputation, and overall risk tolerance of the lender?

The companies that I worked with over the years were constantly in default, most commonly because of financial reporting requirements they weren't hitting. Sending monthly financials in forty-five days instead of thirty days, for example, or not getting financial audits on time, etc. Occasionally, more serious things were happening, like financial covenant defaults, payment default (not paying the required monthly principal and interest), or making an acquisition involving decent amounts of cash without telling us or getting approval first.

The literal interpretation of the legal documents would flag all the above issues the same, as events of default. But most lenders are more interested in real risk versus what might be perceived risk; most lenders are pragmatic. Financial reporting delays are commonplace. Running a start-up is an exercise of putting out the latest fire, and sometimes financials are delayed. Lenders understand that. If they have a good working relationship with the portfolio company and the business is performing, these minor issues aren't a problem. If a company barely missed a financial covenant but in general everything else is going directionally well, then the lender will likely waive the covenant violation and everyone carries on.

Even with some more serious issues, if the company is otherwise doing well—or at least has lots of cash remaining and the board remains supportive—most lenders are willing to be accommodative. As the degree of the violation gets more serious, lenders may be flexible but also add in new ongoing constraints on the business, ask for additional compensation, or a mix of both. If there is significant real risk with a portfolio company, lenders can start taking more drastic actions if warranted. Usually, this is with the hopes of getting the company back on track, but occasionally, actions could focus on ensuring the lender is repaid some or, hopefully, all its principal.

The Company Legal Perspective

One of the consistent trends you see with companies that successfully navigate an event of default is early and frequent communication with their lender. While management may be reluctant to notify a lender early of a potential issue or expected breach, raising potential issues with a lender early will both demonstrate that management is focused on the matter giving rise to the potential breach and provide time for the borrower and lender to find a solution to the matter, whether that is a waiver, an amendment, or possibly more drastic measures. Often, a lender will need time to approve the outcome, and beginning discussions early will provide the lender and borrower room to reach an acceptable solution. It reinforces a solid level of trust with your lender, which can be critical when working through a future or more material breach or default.

Related: If a lender is willing to waive a default or other breach of the loan agreement, it is in the company's interest to get an acknowledgment of that waiver in writing (even if there is otherwise commercial

*agreement between the parties). A waiver or amendment can be infor-
mal or formal, but it should be documented in writing. Most loan agreements include language that explicitly state any waiver is only effective
to the extent it is writing.*

MATERIALLY ADVERSE CHANGE (MAC) CLAUSES

Oh boy, if I had a nickel for every time I had to discuss, define, or
debate a MAC clause, I'd be a wealthy guy. This is one of the most
hotly debated points during the term sheet stage and through full
legal document negotiations. Why? A MAC clause is called a *subjective default*—it is up to the lender to decide what event or action by
a portfolio company is both "material" (meaningful) and "adverse"
(negatively impacts the business). There is no specific event or action it
defines, and depending on a lender's risk tolerance, what constitutes a
MAC default will vary.

Every lender who has been in this industry for a full business cycle
has grappled with whether to use a MAC clause to call a default. Every
investor who has been around for a full business cycle likely has a hor-
ror story of dealing with a lender who is threatening to call a MAC
default and the subsequent fallout thereafter. Odds are you will have a
subjective default of some form in your legal agreement; most lenders
won't do a deal without one. This puts an even finer point on choosing
the right lending partner for your situation. It will always come down
to the people involved and the ties they have woven. The legal agreement, while important, doesn't really matter when compared to the
quality of the relationship between parties.

Now that I've done a solid job undercutting the importance of
the legal process, I'll turn the pen back over to Laurie at DLA Piper,
who was kind enough to lay out the original thought process behind
a MAC clause.

The Lender Legal Perspective

Material adverse change clauses have been around in credit agreements since the 1970s, as opposed to investor support or investor abandonment clauses, which started to appear in lieu of MAC clauses more recently. Why do lenders need them? To protect the lender against unforeseen events that could impair a borrower's ability to repay the loan. A lender can covenant around what they understand and can predict with any portfolio company, but the MAC clause is really about what they can't anticipate. What are the unknowns, what are the curveballs, what's coming out of left field?

There are typically three key components or "prongs" of a MAC clause that are nearly ubiquitous in the venture lending world: (1) a material impairment in the value of the collateral (assets of the company) (2) a material adverse change in the business (operations) of the company and (3) a material impairment in the prospect of repayment of the loan, any of which, if they occur, will cause a "MAC" under the loan document.

MAC definitions and clauses are carefully crafted based on a number of factors including the experiences each lender has had in the market and the circumstances that they want to avoid. Most lenders will not negotiate their MAC clause, period. On very rare occasions, select lenders MAY agree to make very minor changes to their preferred definition, if absolutely necessary for some bespoke reason on a particular high-value transaction, but that is a VERY limited exception to the general "no negotiation" rule.

All of that said, regardless of the negotiated language, US courts have historically been reluctant to allow lenders to call a default based solely on a MAC clause unless the adverse change is significant, long-lasting and fundamentally affects the borrower's ability to perform its obligations. In addition, it has been my experience that many lenders have historically been loath to call MAC defaults except in cases of absolute last resort because of the potential for long-lasting reputational damage.

That said, it remains an option that is available to lenders and past per-formance cannot be relied upon as a measure of future behavior.

The Company Legal Perspective

Although lenders are reluctant to change or negotiate a proposed MAC clause, there are a couple of components of a MAC definition that a borrower may be able to negotiate. The first is related to a material change in the "prospects" of the business operations. Inclusion of the word "prospects" creates even more subjectivity in an already subjective standard and can often be negotiated out. The second relates to the lender determining, based on available information, that the borrower is likely to breach a financial covenant in a future reporting period. This can potentially be removed given that it conflicts with the traditional notion of a financial covenant—a financial covenant is breached as of the measurement date. Although sometimes proposed by lenders, it is not customary to include a potential future breach of a financial cove-nant in the definition of MAC.

Since lenders are not keen to negotiate or change their MAC language, what can a company possibly change here? Some lenders are willing to swap out a broad MAC for a more narrowly defined one, but still subjective default, called an *investor abandonment clause*. More detail on that in the next section. For early-stage venture debt deals with lots of lender interest, it is possible one or more lenders may be willing to strike a MAC entirely if they like the company enough and have worked with the investors on the cap table repeatedly. However, that happens less these days because of the pain that comes during the next deal to the same company when the lender will want to add a MAC back in the deal structure. For later-stage transactions, it is possible that private credit funds may be willing to drop a MAC from their documents if they also have meaningful financial covenants in the deal. Their thinking is that the financial covenants give them more than enough downside protection, and if the company was in compliance with the financial covenants, the odds that a lender would call a MAC default are exceptionally low.

For a MAC or an investor abandonment clause (which we dig into next), you should ask each lender about their internal process for calling a subjective default. At the four venture banks I worked at over the years, that process was robust given the magnitude of the potential reputational damage in the market. Lenders won't likely share the exact specifics but seeing how they articulate their firm's thinking on the topic should be informative and may help color your decision on what lender to partner with.

INTERMISSION

Congratulations! You've officially made it halfway through the longest chapter of the book. Rather than overwhelm you with too much good stuff all at once, I'm offering you a short break in the form of an intermission. What is an intermission? Back in the day, theaters paused halfway through a film so the projectionist could switch reels (teeing up the second half of the movie) and to allow patrons to buy another bag of popcorn or use the bathroom. I've decided to do the same in book form. Feel free to take a short break to do any of the following:

- Stretch

- Refill your coffee or tea

- Text your lawyer

- Use the bathroom, particularly helpful for those of us over forty

- Google "material adverse change clause" or "Did theaters actually have intermissions?"

Back? Refreshed? Excellent. The MAC, investor abandonment and contingency funding clauses are some of the densest AND most negotiated topics in venture lending. I'm glad to have you back and ready to press on.

INVESTOR ABANDONMENT CLAUSE

I'm going to remove all pretense and just let Laurie, Sam and Eric drive the conversation . . .

The Lender Legal Perspective

Investor support clauses arrived in the venture debt market about ten years ago, circa 2015, as an answer to borrower or founder discomfort with the idea of a subjective default being included in a legal agreement, particularly when lending money to very early-stage cash-burning businesses. In those types of businesses, changes happen all the time; those companies pivot regularly because a product doesn't work as planned, customers churn, regulatory approvals can be delayed and companies get close to zero cash—a lot.

In addition, there were a few private credit fund venture lenders that won market share by eliminating the MAC default in their documents, usually when they had heavy financial covenants on the deal they felt they could rely upon instead.

The combination of those two things—a handful of lenders not having a MAC clause and cash-burning businesses that didn't want the MAC—encouraged certain lenders to find another path. That desire for a middle ground is what created the investor support clause, *which will look something like, "If the existing investors refuse to continue to fund the borrower in the amounts and time frame necessary to enable the borrower to satisfy the obligations as they become due and payable..." the lender can cite the investor support clause to stop funding and exercise rights and remedies including potentially accelerating the loan.*

What constitutes continued support? Equity that gives the company a year of runway? Three months? One month? Like with the MAC, most lenders carefully craft their specific investor support clauses based on past experience and their internal credit policy. Even with the narrowed focus of the investor support or abandonment clauses there will be disagreement about what actions investors need to take to be considered supportive. Regardless of whether a deal has a MAC or investor support clause, most venture lenders will want a subjective default in the legal documents when lending to early-stage cash-burning businesses as protection against uncertainty.

The Company Legal Perspective

We see some board members and investors feel very strongly about the MAC clause. Venture bank lenders, especially for smaller deals, have often offered up the investor abandonment clause instead. In effect, it is a narrower version of a MAC clause. It is a meaningful point for many investors and lenders because at least now there is a narrowing of the potential subjective default. Occasionally, we see an investor abandonment clause that requires an investor to provide a written commitment of its continued intent to fund the borrower. In our view, this is not market and not something that a company should agree to because, practically, investors are not going to deliver that type of letter. You don't want to create a scenario that the company or board can't fulfill from the start. Additionally, a company will want an investor abandonment clause to focus on the company's ability to raise capital in the amounts and at the time necessary to repay the loan obligations. In other words, since a venture lender is often looking at a company's ability to raise capital as the source of repayment of a venture loan, the company should look to tailor the investor abandonment clause to address that risk. In today's market, you're likely to have either an investor abandonment or a MAC in every deal, and as the loan size grows, it will almost always be a full MAC clause.

I was around at SVB when the venture-lending market started to incorporate investor abandonment language in lieu of a broader MAC. Ironically, there has been some pushback in the past few years from certain board members to move back toward a broader MAC.

Why? Some investors didn't like the focus the investor abandonment language puts on their ongoing support. In essence, they think if a lender calls an investor abandonment default, that lender is essentially implying to the company that it was the investor(s) fault, and they are the reason the lender is taking action. Taken together, your mileage may vary when talking to board members about what subjective default language they prefer based on their historical experience.

When is it possible to remove both clauses from a legal agreement and avoid having a subjective event of default in the first place? Again, with later-stage venture debt where there will likely be multiple financial covenants, you may be able to negotiate with lenders to remove a subjective default in total, since the financial covenants already give the lender substantial downside protection. The other time frame where you may be able to negotiate out a subjective default is after raising an oversubscribed early-stage equity round from a group of top-tier investors. If you are in that position when bringing on venture debt, some lenders may be willing to remove a MAC or investor abandonment entirely, based on the momentum and quality of the investor syndicate involved. Make sure your board is supportive and aware of your desire to remove a subjective default, because you will likely need their advocacy during their diligence calls with lenders.

CONTINGENCY FUNDING CLAUSE

The MAC and investor abandonment clause are both official events of default; even after the venture debt facility has been fully advanced, these clauses can be used to potentially call everybody back to the table and even prompt the lender to act if warranted. The *contingency funding clause* is not an event of default; it essentially says that if there are undrawn amounts on the venture debt loan prior to any advance request being funded, the lender can confirm that a MAC has not occurred. And if the lender determines that a MAC has occurred, it is within the scope of the legal agreement to decline to advance the remaining amount of the debt. This is still a very significant step for a lender to take but it is not technically the same as calling an event of default. A company may still have an outstanding balance with the lender that can stay in place as agreed but allows the lender the right not to advance further dollars. Back to Laurie at DLA Piper:

The Lender Legal Perspective

As mentioned earlier, the reason why the lender wants a subjective default is to protect against the unknown. Funding contingencies allow a lender not to fund a requested draw if the lender believes that a MAC has occurred, there is a lack of investor support, or both. The lender is not requiring the company to pay back everything that is borrowed or taking any other action, but they want to pause and fully understand the plan going forward because some underlying assumptions have significantly changed.

A common example would be that a company has lost a large amount of revenue because they were concentrated with one major customer who just churned. Perhaps that lost customer also has the lender questioning whether the company will be able to access equity capital (i.e., investor support). The funding contingency allows lenders to take a pause to reevaluate, talk with all parties, including the board, and potentially negotiate a path forward.

The Company Legal Perspective

Some lenders will propose to expand the contingency funding clause to also include other prongs, in addition to a requirement that no MAC has occurred. For example, some lenders will propose that as a condition of funding, no MAC has occurred and there has been no material adverse deviation from the company's budget and projections. Arguably, this latter prong adds objectivity to the contingency funding clause, but it only does so for the benefit of the lender. To the extent possible, a company should try to avoid a contingency funding clause that is based on performance to plan as it, in effect, becomes an additional financial covenant. Although it may not trigger an event of default, the company may not be able to borrow when it expects to be able to do so.

All lenders will have a contingency funding clause in some form within their legal documents; whether it will be referenced in the term sheet depends on the level of depth and transparency each lender covers in their boilerplate proposal. Unlike a MAC or investor abandonment clause, a company can avoid any issues with contingency funding by drawing down the full balance of the venture debt at close of documentation. That obviously comes with an economic cost, but I've seen plenty of portfolio companies get comfortable with that trade-off over the years. They wanted certainty that the funds would be there when needed and they got that—by drawing down at close.

COLLATERAL

This language defines the type of lien a lender would like to put in place and the specific parts of the business that will be included under that lien as *collateral*. You may see this section alternatively referred to as *security* or *lien*. Only a few major variables exist for most venture debt transactions and the most frequently used version will look like this: *First-priority lien on all assets with a negative pledge on intellectual property (IP)*. First priority means the lender will be the first creditor, other than statutory obligations, to be repaid from the company's assets in any scenario. This is also known as being a *senior lender*. A *junior lender* or *second-lien lender* are scenarios where a private credit fund might take a second-priority lien and sit behind another capital provider. We will cover the nuances of having a senior and a junior lender in an upcoming section.

Let's take a pause to quickly talk about the order of priority or the liquidation waterfall when a company fails. This determines who gets paid in what order, assuming there are funds or assets available. The first group to be paid are statutory obligations holders that include accrued PTO and sick time of employees, for example. This does vary a bit state by state, but most lenders and investors are not going to be eager to stiff employees if at all avoidable. The second group to be paid are secured creditors. This is where venture lenders sit. If there is more than one lender, the order of their liens will determine who is paid first, second, third, etc. This group could also include bondholders or convertible note holders, if they are secured; you see convertible notes fairly often in Start-Up Land. If notes are secured—a rare occurrence—venture lenders will require the noteholders to subordinate their security interest, meaning they agree to be paid after the venture debt is repaid in full. The third group to be paid out are any administrative expenses related to a bankruptcy process and unsecured priority claims like unpaid taxes. The fourth group paid out are unsecured creditors that include vendors (accounts payable), leaseholders, bondholders (if unsecured), and convertible noteholders (also if unsecured). The last group to be paid in a liquidation are equity holders, and within this group, there is also a set pecking order. Preferred shareholders (venture capital firms and sometimes founders) are first with . . . drum roll please . . . common shareholders (employees) paid last. Now back to what the *collateral* section in a term sheet means.

The words *all assets* are very literal in this case and include cash, accounts receivables, equipment, etc. The only exception or carve-out being made is the *negative pledge on IP*, which means that the lender will not take a security interest in the company's intellectual property. Asking for a negative pledge in this case means the lender is also prohibiting the company from allowing any other party to take a security interest in the IP as well. This is sometimes referred to as a double negative pledge.

Seems a bit odd, doesn't it? Most start-ups have a small list of assets and what cash they have tends to shrink month over month. It would seem the only thing of real potential value is the IP that the company is building or creating. So why is the market norm to exclude IP from the otherwise all-encompassing lien on the company's assets? Laurie at DLA Piper has the answer.

The Lender Legal Perspective

The practice of having a negative pledge on IP goes back forty years to the start of venture lending. Companies and entrepreneurs considered their source code, a type of IP, to be the "crown jewels," or the most valuable asset in the business. Founders were therefore extremely sensitive about letting lenders put a lien on their most valuable asset, or really their only true asset, outside of the cash that they raised and A/R if they had a little bit of revenue.

As a compromise, many lenders said "You don't have to give us a lien on the IP. We'll only take the cash, the A/R, and all other assets," but that comes with two big caveats. First, the company can't give anyone else a lien on the IP, and second, the lender gets a lien on the proceeds of the sale of the IP (whether this is enforceable or not if the IP is not part of the collateral is beyond the scope of this discussion).

When agreeing to rely on a negative pledge, prudent lenders will confirm that the related covenants in the credit documentation are properly crafted. For instance, venture lenders will typically include a "double negative pledge" covenant that prohibits the borrower from granting a negative pledge on its intellectual property to third parties to ensure it can later take security in the borrower's intellectual property without triggering a default under the borrower's other agreements.

Additionally, lenders take care to ensure that the borrower is not able to use the disposition or asset sale covenant to dispose of material intellectual property that it would be unable to finance due to the negative pledge. Lenders may pay particular attention for potential loopholes when a borrower has (or could in the future have) subsidiaries that are not loan parties under the credit facility. As a result of this concern, "immaterial subsidiaries" or similar non-loan parties are often prohibited from owning material intellectual property.

Lastly, lenders may want to confirm that the obligations secured by the borrower's collateral would include any potential judgment for breach of contract resulting from the borrower's violation of the negative pledge. If covered (and assuming the value of the borrower's collateral exceeds the amount owed to the lender), the lender may be able to exercise remedies against the borrower's other assets to satisfy its judgment. This determination may hinge on the loan agreement's indemnification and expense reimbursement provisions, which courts often interpret narrowly, so clarity is key.

The Company Legal Perspective

In addition to potentially preserving the value of IP for founders or equity investors, excluding IP from the collateral securing a venture debt loan can have a practical benefit in a workout scenario or bankruptcy since the company will have an unencumbered asset. In a workout scenario, the company may be able to grant the venture lender a lien on IP in exchange for an amendment or waiver. Similarly, in a bankruptcy scenario, a company may be able to use unencumbered IP to secure debtor-in-possession (DIP) financing. While a company may not be able to exclude IP from collateral in all deals, especially as deal sizes increase, keeping a potentially valuable asset unencumbered can give a company a position to negotiate from in a down scenario.

Lenders may tweak what collateral they ask for as part of their venture debt proposal; instead of a negative pledge on IP, they might do the opposite and ask to have IP as part of their collateral pool from the start. As referenced, this typically happens in later-stage transactions as the debt quantums get larger, and in a lender's mind, the increased size of the debt justifies taking a lien on IP from the start. Occasionally, you may see lenders include a performance milestone where, if the company falls below a certain level of performance, the collateral position changes from a negative pledge on IP to IP being added to the collateral pool. This is called a "springing" lien on IP.

More frequently, lenders will accommodate the corporate structure or the sensitivities of their potential portfolio company and be willing to "carve out" a portion of the company's assets from the collateral pool. If there are international subsidiaries with limited assets, for example, lenders may consider leaving those out of the collateral pool. If the company wants to finance some portion of their equipment (e.g. servers) with specific vendor financing, typically the cheapest and most flexible option, lenders may be willing to allow for that with some sort of upper dollar limit. The specific needs of any company will vary, but know that lenders are willing to at least consider making modifications to their collateral pool when justified.

SENIOR AND JUNIOR LIEN POSITIONS

One of the bigger differences between private credit funds and venture banks is the former group's willingness to take a second-lien or *junior lender* position. Venture banks will always ask to be a senior lender and in the first-lien position; this is driven by regulatory requirements and market norms. Since banks always are the first secured lender, this is also one of the reasons their debt tends to cost less. Private credit funds, not being nearly as regulated, end up in a junior position quite frequently, especially if a company already has a line of credit, small piece of venture debt, or equipment financing from a bank. The private credit fund will say, *Great! Keep all that in place and we will provide our capital with a junior lien.* This also happens to be a justification for the increased cost of the debt since they will get repaid after the bank. Why would a company want to deal with two lenders, though? A couple of reasons. The quantum of debt the company can bring on will likely be greater than what they can get from one lender alone. The blended cost of capital between the cheaper bank financing and the more expensive private credit financing can also be attractive. Having two lenders may also enable the company to more easily upsize the debt over time since both capital providers each have their own funding sources.

When two or more lenders are providing capital to the same company, they must agree on how they will work together. This is done partially by holding different lien positions, but also by a document called an *inter-creditor agreement*. That agreement outlines the rules of engagement between both lenders. A number of hypothetical situations are addressed up front to avoid conflict down the road, such as if the company is in default with one lender but not the other. If the company is in default with the junior lender specifically, how much notice or time does the senior lender get until the junior lender can act? How much debt can the senior lender provide to the company beyond the current level? These are common sticking points between banks and private credit funds when they share a portfolio company.

Before you run out and decide to take on debt from two lenders, it is worth considering all the pros and cons. We've already discussed the bulk of the benefits: lower blended cost of capital than taking only venture debt from one lender, deeper pockets, and ease of upsizing from both in the future. The downsides are that you now have to manage two distinct parties—sending ongoing reporting to both the bank and the private credit fund as well as regular company updates for each group. Depending on how the company is performing, it is possible you may have differing views between lenders on the riskiness of the situation. That can get messy very quickly. If, at the end of the day, the benefits outweigh the risks and you move forward with a senior and junior lender, incorporate the following into your thinking:

Historical working relationship. Confirm with both the bank and private credit fund that they have worked together in a senior and junior context previously. Ideally, they've done so frequently and navigated through a market cycle together. Trust, but verify, what they are saying by asking your outside counsel if they have seen these two lenders partner up before. Do reference checks with portfolio companies listed on each lender's website. Find portfolio companies where you have shared investors or second connections on LinkedIn, then reach out directly. You are more likely to get candid feedback than with intros from the lenders directly.

Negotiate for flexibility on the senior indebtedness cap. This is a common sticking point in the inter-creditor agreement between senior and junior lenders. Even though the agreement is between both lenders, it has a meaningful direct impact on the portfolio company. Junior lenders understandably want to limit how much debt sits ahead of them, because as the senior debt increases, it will be harder for the junior lender to be repaid in a downside scenario. So junior lenders typically want an upper limit on the amount of the senior debt. Most private credit funds will ask to set the senior debt cap at the current senior debt amount or perhaps with a little cushion or headroom.

At the company, I'd encourage you to consider what kind of working capital needs you may have in twelve to twenty-four months. Try to incorporate that thinking into setting the right senior debt cap. If things are generally going okay or better down the road, private credit funds may be willing to relax/increase the senior debt cap, but it will likely come with some kind of new fee or warrant. If things aren't going well, a private credit fund may come back with a hard "no" and the company is either forced to take more capital from the private credit fund or perhaps even forced to bring on equity. A company's best leverage point to get the senior debt cap set appropriately is during term sheet negotiations.

It is also worth contemplating the ability to add junior debt down the road when putting senior debt in place. Most credit agreements will require the senior lender's permission to do so. It will be approved most of the time as long as the junior debt is subordinated. But if you think it's possible your company may want or need junior debt in the future, it's worth discussing early; even if the legal agreement isn't adjusted, you'll have a sense of the likelihood your senior lender will approve down the road.

Confirm whether the junior debt cross-defaults to senior debt financial covenants. Senior bank debt, particularly lines of credit, tends to have financial covenants that measure the ongoing performance of the business. Junior venture debt tends not to have financial covenants. That lack of structure is what allows venture debt to truly extend runway and also helps justify the economic cost. Most private credit funds include a cross-default section in their legal documents; if the company is in default with the senior lender, the junior lender is also able to call a default. This makes sense when covering more egregious events of default, like a company no longer making regular payments. However, what you want to be clear about—and hopefully avoid—is the cross-default becoming a back door for the junior lender to get the benefits or risk mitigation that the senior lender's financial covenants provide. At that point, you are basically paying a lot for debt that doesn't extend runway. Negotiate early to have the cross-default carve out financial covenants on the senior debt, if any. You'll thank me later.

8

OTHER COMPONENTS OF THE TERM SHEET

Every lender will have a *term sheet expiration,* or expiry date at or near the back of their term sheet. Some lenders will also include a *closing time frame* that sets a clock on how long the deal will take to close after execution of the term sheet. I've had several founders, CEOs, or CFOs worried about running up against both types of dates on my term sheets or dates that have been set by other lenders. Those founders, CEOs, or CFOs were equating them to the same expiry dates they'd seen in venture capital term sheets. While they are functionally the same, dates in venture-lending term sheets matter less.

The main reason they are included is to protect a lender from deterioration in a company's performance if a lengthy amount of time passes during term sheet negotiations or the legal process. Over the years, every lender has had on-again, off-again discussions with prospective borrowers. The lender will issue a term sheet and not hear anything from the company for weeks or months, or perhaps some initial dialogue and then radio silence. Then, several months later, that same company comes back and wants to rekindle the debt discussion. Or even more comical, not hearing from that company for months and then getting an email that includes a signed term sheet in their inbox. Nine times out of ten, the company's performance has faltered or they were unable to get better terms from others. Lenders may still be willing to provide capital, but if they do, it will likely come with structural and economic changes. Hence, the expiry date. It protects the lender from reputational damage of "not honoring the term sheet" when significant time has passed.

The other reason some lenders like to have an expiry date in their term sheet is to put pressure on the company to sign the document. The time frame will be set intentionally short to manufacture a sense of urgency. If you are evaluating term sheets from various lenders, just know that this is gamesmanship. You shouldn't feel any real pressure from a term sheet expiration date or closing time frame; operate at whatever pace is appropriate for the business.

MARKETING

There is nothing a lender wants to do more than issue a press release or tombstone bragging about a deal they just closed with an amazing new portfolio company. You will likely find a section in most term sheets where the lender is asking permission to talk publicly about the lending relationship they have with your company. It might look something like, *"Borrower grants Lender the right to use the Borrower's logo in marketing materials, issue a tombstone and a press release upon close of documentation."* Marketing of the deal is particularly good for the lender, but it can also be good for a company. Similar to the close of a venture capital round, a large new debt deal can speak to the increased scale and size of the business, now with an even bigger war chest.

However, taking on debt isn't always something companies want to discuss publicly, or at least not the specifics of the transaction. And sometimes, the situation just isn't all that rosy. The marketing section is a "nice to have" for lenders and you can certainly negotiate it out of a deal with little effort. Middle ground I found that worked for most of my portfolio companies was the ability to use the company's logo in marketing materials, but never to talk about the specifics of what we did with the company.

If you are a later-stage company with public aspirations, consider that the specifics of any debt on the balance sheet will come out when the S-1 filing is released. So, getting ahead of that with your lender to decide whether and how to discuss publicly can be time well spent.

CLOSING CONDITIONS

Typically, near or at the end of a term sheet, each lender will outline *closing conditions* or *subject to*'s. These are items that need to happen after execution of the term sheet but before closing the transaction. Whether they are explicitly listed or not, every lender needs to complete any remaining diligence, finalize their internal underwriting, and get internal credit or investment committee approval. Further, every venture debt transaction will also be subject to satisfactory legal documentation. If the lender has not talked with board members yet, investor calls will be listed as a closing condition. If there are any specific events or milestones that must occur prior to closing, they may end up listed in this section as well. Something like, *Subject to Borrower closing on a minimum of $10,000,000 in net cash proceeds as part of a Series A equity round on or before 6/15/202X.* Another item that we just recently covered, the contingency funding clause, may be referenced here as a *subject to* before every advance or draw down on the venture debt.

How often are lenders unable to close a deal because of subject to's? Or more controversially, how often will lenders use closing condition items to back out of a deal? Not often, but it does happen occasionally. Lenders will do everything they can to avoid the reputational impact of not delivering or being perceived as having "pulled a term sheet." They will drag their feet, hoping the company decides to walk. They might try to renegotiate the deal and increase structure or the economic cost, hoping either the company walks or they actually get a better risk-adjusted structure if the company still decides to move forward. If you've chosen a reputable lender, the odds of this happens after signing the term sheet is low.

CONFIDENTIALITY

Language somewhere in the term sheet will state that the company is not allowed to share said document or the specifics of it with any party who is not a direct employee of the business, a board member, or others on a need-to-know basis (like advisers, lawyers, etc.), without the prior written consent of the lender. In my entire venture-lending career, I have never been asked by a company for approval to share a term sheet with others. Though strangely, I have been on the receiving end of a copious number of term sheets from other lenders—if not the actual term sheets, I was often privy to the board decks that included a stack ranked grid of all the lenders, their terms, economics, etc.

While a confidentiality clause is included in everybody's term sheet, most lenders are pragmatic and realize that information is likely going to be shared. It's typically not a problem unless a term sheet gets out to the broader public or on social media. That would quickly draw the ire of a venture lender. Try to be a good steward of the work these firms have put in and don't share information unless truly necessary.

EXCLUSIVITY AND NO-SHOP CLAUSE

A *no-shop clause* is common in M&A transactions and most venture capital term sheets frequently have them although it's a little less common in venture debt, particularly from venture banks. But an entrepreneur may see the no-shop clause a little when dealing with private credit funds.

The language would read something like, *Borrower agrees that until the 30th day from the execution of this term sheet it will not (a) solicit or entertain any proposal, (b) negotiate with any other provider, or (c) provide any information with respect to Borrower to any provider who might be expected to propose alternate financing, or Borrower shall pay Lender an amount equal to the Facility Fee and any then outstanding legal costs.* This example provides for a thirty-day exclusivity period for the lender to work on closing the deal with the borrower. You may also see forty-five- or sixty-day time frames as well.

I've always operated under the assumption that it was my responsibility and my team's responsibility to win a company's business up until the deal closed. If I needed to have an exclusivity period in place to help enforce good behavior, I'd already lost the battle. If a company found a deal from a partner they liked better, even after signing my term sheet, I'd wish them well and think about what I could have done differently. At the same time, it sucks to get to a place where a company has signed your term sheet and then takes a deal from a different party. It doesn't happen very frequently, but when it does, trust me, the burned lender will remember the company and investors involved for a long time. Realize that if you decide to walk away after signing a term sheet, you may be on the hook for some of the fees and costs that lender has incurred, but more critically, you are burning a bridge in the process. Choose wisely or just negotiate harder up front before signing anyone's term sheet.

CASE STUDY

SURPRISES ARE ONLY GOOD FOR
BIRTHDAYS AND ANNIVERSARIES—PHONE TAP

This is the only case study where I've chosen to anonymize the company and those involved, outside of myself. The outcome was not fun for anyone, so I'm attempting to share the story and lessons learned without throwing further salt in the wound.

"Marshall, I want to see you in person at your office in San Francisco tomorrow at 10 a.m." That was it—there was nothing else in the email, no context; it was just that one line. I responded to ask what he wanted to talk about and the CEO said he wanted to talk about what had just happened between the company and SVB. The tone was ominous. Given the situation, I invited my boss at the time, SVB's Head of Northern California, and a senior partner from our advisory services team to join. That team gets involved in any meaningful downside situation.

The next day, the founder came in, sat down, and for fifty-eight minutes of the hour-long meeting he looked straight at me without acknowledging the others in the room and said a variety of the following paraphrased statements:

> "Marshall, you should never be in a position to make a decision about lending or banking ever again."

> "You should not be leading people anywhere."

> "I will make sure that you never work anywhere else and my investors will know your name."

> "You're a stain on Silicon Valley and you shouldn't be trusted."

There was no constructive conversation or discussion about how to navigate the ongoing liquidity issues the company was experiencing.

I had become the convenient punching bag for the founder of a business that hadn't yet found its footing after more than a decade and was facing a very uncertain equity fundraise. At the end of the hour, he got up and silently walked out of our office.

A month earlier, I had been promoted to director (hooray!) and had taken over a team of four other lenders based in SVB's Palo Alto office. My new team was focused on mid- and later-stage hardware companies. This was in the early 2010s, when hardware was not nearly as sexy as it is today. I carried over a few portfolio companies from my previous team, but the majority of the portfolio companies on the team I now led were new to me. I spent most of that first month getting up to speed on the portfolio, particularly the best companies and the riskiest situations. "Phone Tap" was one of the latter.

They had been in business for more than a decade, raised more than $75M in venture capital, and had revenues in the millions. The challenge was they were still burning a decent amount of cash and trying to put together a Series E financing. The company was also, ironically, not entirely new to me. They had been a portfolio company and borrower of a bank I'd worked at before SVB. Because of that, I knew the company's track record and some of its history while also getting the current state of play. We were concerned that existing equity investors were tapped out. The funds involved were each more than ten years old and there had already been several insider bridge equity rounds. My team was due for an update call with the company to get the latest on the business but also, more importantly, the ongoing fundraise.

The night before the official business update call, the CFO of Phone Tap called the Vice President on my new team, who was the lead on the relationship. The CFO told him that the equity fundraise was not going well and that the company would likely have to file an *assignment for benefit of creditors* (ABC for short) on Monday. ABCs are a less costly way to shut down or hand over the remains of a business to its creditors or lender. Even though we already suspected things weren't going great, whenever a portfolio company tells you it is potentially shutting down in less than a week, you pay attention. The RM texted me that night to let me know the unfortunate news. The next day (Friday), I joined the official update call with my VP and the CFO at Phone Tap. The CFO confirmed again that the equity fundraise had not been trending well, gave a quick snapshot of the business, and talked about a couple of large customer invoices that were taking longer to pay. He then abruptly said that the company wanted to borrow an additional $3M against those customer invoices. Without that cash, he said, Phone Tap would likely need to shut down the following week. The RM and I exchanged a glance . . . did he just say he wanted to advance new money? As the senior member of SVB on the call, I told the CFO we would need to get some more information including touching base with investors before we'd be able to fund their drawdown request. He understood and said he'd be happy to put together any detail we needed. Then we ended the call.

A quick summary of the debt Phone Tap had with SVB: We had funded numerous venture debt facilities over the prior four years. There was approximately $3M of venture debt outstanding that was slowly being repaid. The venture debt did not have any further dollars available. We also had a line of credit in place that was used to borrow against the company's accounts receivable. That line of credit had $2M outstanding with another $3M of availability. This line of credit was structured so that the company could borrow against customer invoices (A/R), but once each invoice was paid by the end customer, the outstanding balance on the line of credit would also need to be repaid shortly thereafter; the line of credit was expected to be used for short-term working capital needs, not to extend runway.

We were able to schedule calls with the two main investors. These firms were the two largest outside shareholders in the business, the longest tenured investors, and both held board seats. Each firm was well known and respected in Silicon Valley. We knew the individuals well, having talked with each of them numerous times about Phone Tap and other portfolio companies over the years. Both partners confirmed what we had already suspected: the Series E fundraise was not looking good and there was no meaningful progress to find a new outside lead investor for the round. We let each investor know that we would be willing to advance new dollars on the line of credit if they came in alongside us with additional equity of a similar amount. We didn't want to be the last money in alone, given the state of the business.

Unfortunately, both board members confirmed that they did not have the capacity or willingness within their firms to continue to support the business. In my experience, it's rare to hear that so explicitly from investors, and whether or not we advanced new money, it seemed like the company's fate was sealed.

After internal deliberations taking in the entirety of the situation, we decided that without continued support from investors, the lack of progress on raising outside equity, and near-term cash out, we were not comfortable allowing further advances on the line of credit without additional requirements, effectively using our contingency funding clause without officially noticing the company as such.

We talked with the CFO and CEO at Phone Tap early the next week. We let them know that we would be willing to advance more money if the existing investors put in more capital alongside us or an outside investor provided a term sheet for the Series E. Other than those two paths, we were not comfortable advancing any more debt. That message was not well received and led to the infamous meeting shortly thereafter with yours truly getting yelled at for the better part of an hour.

AFTERMATH

Phone Tap started to unwind shortly after the meeting where the founder and CEO read me the riot act. No Series E round came together. The existing investor syndicate did not put in additional capital and the company pivoted to an asset sale run by a third-party firm that specialized in wind-down situations. As it turned out, the company's IP portfolio, as one of the first movers in its space, had some value. Two components of the business found buyers. Unfortunately, the rest of the business went to zero. Employees were laid off and equity value for common stockholders went to zero. The asset sale generated enough for SVB as the senior lienholder to be fully repaid, plus another $5M, give or take, going to preferred shareholders.

KEY TAKEAWAYS

Don't surprise your lender. Telling your lender that you may shut down within a week without borrowing more capital is not the right order of operations. You ideally want to have had a lengthy ongoing dialogue for months. Everyone needs to know the state of the business and the continuing fundraise in near real time. That might seem like overkill or a lot of work; it also might seem like you are giving your lender the opportunity to take harsh action sooner. The reality, though, is that if you have chosen your lending partner well, they should be more comfortable because they have the full picture. They may also be able to help navigate the situation proactively before cash levels get near zero. Once you are close to or at zero, there is no more runway to potentially provide help. That is what happened with Phone Tap.

We could have shared our concerns. I had only been leading my new team for forty-five days when this all happened, but we suspected the company's fundraise was not going well from the moment I reviewed the portfolio with my new team. In hindsight, we could have proactively shared our concern with the company and board sooner. I'm not sure that would have changed the ultimate outcome, but it would have at least given us a bit more time to work together to find a better path forward. A lesson for all the lenders out there not to wait for news from your portfolio companies, particularly if the news is likely to be bad. Seek it out.

Alignment between the entrepreneur, board, and lender is critical. We knew from calls with the main investors in Phone Tap that they were at the end of their rope, though it didn't seem like that was being openly discussed in the boardroom with the company. Or if it was, it certainly wasn't heard by the founder. This led to the company hitting the wall the way it did. Had the board been aligned, perhaps there could have been a softer landing for the company (full acquisition and a home for employees) and not such a rushed or distressed asset sale.

Entrepreneurship is hard. That was the only time in my career that I'd been used as the proverbial punching bag by a founder. I've had plenty of heated negotiations or disagreements that eventually got resolved, but this one stands out. I don't begrudge the founder for feeling like SVB and me, specifically, had scuttled his business. Building a company from scratch is a monumental undertaking. The highs are HIGH, and the lows are LOW. This was his baby. In the heat of the moment, we were the convenient target to blame. We haven't seen each other or talked since that fateful meeting. I hope he is doing okay in life now and wish him well.

9

RUNNING AN EFFICIENT
LEGAL PROCESS

The longest part of a venture debt fundraise is usually the legal process that follows signing a term sheet; seems only fitting that we address that process in what is one of the shortest chapters in the book. Why the short shrift? Well, the primary legal documents involved—the credit agreement and the warrant agreement—can easily exceed 125 pages by themselves, not to mention all the other ancillary documents that need to be drafted or reviewed by outside counsel on both sides. To cover all of it in depth here would easily double the size of this book and make it a lot less exciting to read. The other reason not to go in depth is the large number of variables that make each individual transaction unique, so generalized perspective or advice won't be as useful.

Good news, though: if you've taken my earlier advice and engaged experienced outside counsel, they will be able to walk you and your company through the legal process better than I can, so this chapter is mostly focused on best practices for working with your counsel, lender, and lender's counsel to successfully close the transaction.

THE PERFECTION CERTIFICATE

Congratulations! You've signed the term sheet for a new venture debt deal from an excellent lending partner. As a reward for taking such a meaningful step, the first thing that the lender or their counsel is going to give you is a lengthy form called a *perfection certificate, collateral information certificate,* or something similar. Regardless of what it is called, this form rivals any government document in its ability to demoralize even the strongest-willed entrepreneur. It is not the most user-friendly way to kick off a legal process, but it is a critical component and source of information that will guide what language and specifics must be included in the loan documents.

So, what is a perfection certificate? It is a questionnaire filled out by the borrower that gives the lender a complete snapshot of the corporate structure, all assets, and current or potential future liabilities. This gives the lender and their counsel the level of detail needed to ensure they are able to accurately take and perfect a security interest in the assets of the business. Hence, *perfection* certificate. Three cheers for literal document names.

The types of questions it asks include where the company is incorporated, where employees are located, how many physical office buildings the company has, whether the company has trademarks, copyrights, or patents, existing bank accounts, any outstanding litigation or other legal issues, etc. As much as you may want to procrastinate working on the perfection certificate given its overwhelming nature, it is in your best interest to get cracking straight away. Perfection certificates can quickly become a gating item to close the transaction. Depending on the specifics that come back in the document (a large IP portfolio, some kind of outstanding litigation, more bank accounts than previously known, etc.), the language in loan documents may need to be updated. It may also affect the lender's willingness to be flexible (or not) during the ongoing legal negotiations. Make the perfection certificate a priority if possible. For early-stage companies with less complexity, the effort needed isn't as robust, but for later-stage companies with more scale, it will take a fair amount of time.

One final motivation for completing the perfection certificate quickly and accurately is that it will be referenced throughout the broader legal documents. Essentially, a company is affirming—known as *representing* and *warranting*—that they've accurately outlined the current size, scope, and complexity of the business. The lender will say everything in the perfection certificate is allowed, but any change or update in the future may require explicit approval, so correcting a mistake can cost you down the road.

Following the perfection certificate, you will encounter the following list of documents, deliverables, and approvals during the average two-month-long legal process:

- Credit Agreement or Loan and Security Agreement: Primary legal document for the transaction. Usually, 100 pages or more.

- Warrant Agreement: Grants the lender the right to buy stock in the future at a set price. Usually 15–20 pages.

- Subordination Agreement(s): If needed to ensure convertible notes or any other secured debt is subordinated to the senior lender.

- Updated Insurance Certificates: General business insurance needs to list the lender as a *lender loss payee.*

- DACAs: For all banking relationships if a private credit fund is the lender; only for secondary banking when borrowing from a venture bank.

- Landlord Waivers: Gives lenders the right to access physical office locations in a very downside scenario.

- Board Resolution: Needed to approve the company taking on debt.

- Preferred Stockholder Approval: If needed for the company to issue new warrants.

BEST PRACTICES

Eric and Sam at Fenwick and Laurie at DLA Piper put together separate lists of best practices for this book. I also wrote down a few items I'd learned from the hundreds of legal processes I've navigated in the past. After reviewing our lists, wouldn't you know it, there were a ton of commonalities. We are sharing those best practices collectively from our combined decades of experience.

Don't be the intermediary. Let the lawyers talk to one another. Yes, lawyers are expensive, but talking only through businesspeople results in a lengthier, more frustrating process. Many founders will think, *If I let the lawyers talk, they're just going to drive up legal costs*, but it's usually the opposite. Partners you trust are going to be succinct and efficient when talking to the other counsel, which often means the people on the business side don't have to be the intermediaries. I (Marshall) was guilty of this kind of gatekeeping earlier in my career, thinking it would be more efficient. It wasn't. Now I give guidance to the counsel I'm working with and then they are free to connect with the company or its counsel as they see fit and just keep the lender and company informed throughout.

Don't let the battle of redlines ensue. Let the lawyers do a turn of the documents and then get on an all-hands call to discuss open issues sooner rather than later so you can narrow down the list of items that people really care about. Humans tend to hide behind their computers and just want to go back-and-forth and ask for the same thing multiple times assuming the outcome will change. Who wants to do that with their lives? It might seem like progress to do this back-and-forth, but it costs more money and makes the process much less efficient. Many people are reluctant to make a phone call—a phone call to an actual person has become a lost art—but that's the way that deals get done, so try not to respond to every single redline with another redline. Get on the phone to get deals done faster.

Focus on your key issues. Talk with your counsel about issues that are specific to your company and ask them to focus on those items with your lender. Don't negotiate on everything because it dilutes what may be truly important and increases costs for limited benefit. Instead, focus your counsel on getting the operational flexibility you need to run the business. If you are looking for flexibility with respect to something that may occur in the future, focus again on the issues that are likely to arise (as opposed to flexibility that simply is nice to have for a hypothetical situation not in the current business plan).

Set your timeline. This is something that many people don't do, but try to set a target closing date and work back from that date to include a calendar for document delivery, redlines, issues list calls, closing deliverables, credit approval, signing, and the official close. If a deal has to close in three weeks, work back from this date. Confirm that counsel will deliver documents to you by date X and you will deliver comments back to counsel by Y, then you will all get on a call on date Z. That will leave three to five days to handle any deliverables that are trailing and credit approvals or remaining items, and here's when everyone expects to sign. You really have to hold people to those deadlines if something has to happen by a certain date.

Be realistic about the timespan of the process. When setting a timeline, expect the process to take forty-five to sixty days and just be thrilled if it gets done in less time. Obviously, everyone wants to move faster than that, but you must set realistic expectations, and forty-five to sixty days should be doable. That means that you have to start immediately on all DACAs, landlord waivers, subordination agreements, and other third-party documents—frequently the barriers to closing on a timely basis—because we, as the two counterparties, don't control those and someone else is involved. Company counsel should deliver drafts of the board and shareholder resolutions early to get those out of the way. Those often become last-minute items for borrowers but could easily be done early in the process. Request loan payoff documents early; if a loan payoff is included in the transaction, it can hold up closing.

Venture debt is a negotiation. Look for compromises that work wherever you can. Both sides should feel like they had to give up some of their points to get other areas they truly wanted. A long-term partnership won't start off the right way if one side feels like they "won." Talk often, text, have your lender and their counsel on speed dial, stay in touch, and make it your priority to communicate early and often. The best lenders don't just sit back on their heels but are focused and driven. The same thing holds true with the best lawyers; they're focused and driven as opposed to waiting for responses, so take advantage of that.

Keep your board informed. While your board (and possibly preferred stockholders) will need to approve the definitive loan documents, it is helpful to keep them (and, if applicable, preferred stockholders) updated throughout the process. This can include the specifics of term sheets that the company is considering and the models shared with the lenders to set any financial covenants. Nothing is worse than going to the board for approval of the final loan documents and receiving feedback that they are not supportive of the transaction. Many investors that serve on boards have experience with venture debt through other portfolio companies and will have a perspective on current market terms or even potential lending partners.

Think about third-party deliverables early. Your counsel will help you with this process, but do not put off workstreams that involve third parties, such as account control agreements, insurance deliverables, landlord waivers, or an inter-creditor/subordination agreement with existing noteholders. Workstreams involving third parties can often become gating items to close, so starting early is particularly helpful to moving a deal forward efficiently.

Review perfection certificates or collateral information certificates. Perfection certificates were mentioned earlier, but it is worth emphasizing that it is helpful to put in time up front preparing or reviewing these certificates as the information listed in them can impact both the terms of a loan agreement and the scope of closing deliverables. If errors or omissions are identified later in the process, it may require revisiting certain terms in the loan documents. Your counsel can help guide you through these disclosure documents. It is worth the time to discuss them with your counsel if you have questions.

Pay attention to the impact of lender warrants. A warrant can trigger specific rights in the company's existing charter and investment documents, such as investor preemptive rights and a preferred stock anti-dilution adjustment, and the issuance of warrants may require specific preferred stock/investor approval. It is important to make sure that any special investor rights triggered by the issuance of the warrants are waived and any warrant-specific approvals are obtained early in the closing process.

10

GET MORE FROM
YOUR LENDING PARTNER

This chapter is focused on how an entrepreneur, CFO, or company can build a more meaningful relationship with their lender. While the primary value of a good lending partner is providing the right amount of capital with the appropriate structure and economics, that is table stakes for any company deciding to take on venture debt. In addition to making day-to-day interactions much more enjoyable, a solid working relationship will provide other tangible benefits. If a lender likes and, more importantly, trusts the team at a portfolio company, their flexibility will be much more likely when the business hits a bump in the road or they will move faster to provide additional capital when the business is ramping. They will work that much harder for the company because of the strength of the relationship. The following are tips to help you build a trust-based relationship with your lender, and a few thoughts on how to put your lender to work on your behalf outside of the debt they already provide.

SHARE THE POSITIVE AND THE NEGATIVE

Building a business is hard. Famous quotes from investors and founders about the gauntlet that is entrepreneurship abound; I'm partial to Elon Musk's "Running a start-up is like staring into the abyss and eating glass." Every lender knows how hard it is because most of the companies they see end up in failure, and every lender I know has ample empathy for founders. They also talk regularly with all kinds of people in the innovation ecosystem including their own portfolio companies, the investors in those companies, other founders, investors, and service providers. Because of that, the best lenders are great at pattern recognition and, by extension, discerning whether someone is giving them the full story (or not).

It is a bit ironic that the way to get a lender more excited and more comfortable with giving you a lot of money is to tell them, in equal measure, about the opportunities *and* the challenges of the business. Lenders know founders are constantly walking around with their hair on fire, jumping from one problem that needs solving to the next. If they don't hear directly from you about what is not working, they have to assume or piece together on their own what challenges the business is facing. As an entrepreneur, don't leave that open to interpretation. Don't hide things that aren't working in the business or that you may not have a solution to. Be direct in sharing information and updates, both good and bad, with your lending partner regularly. This might feel scary at first. *What if they react poorly? What if they think I don't know what I'm doing?* Take a leap of faith and trust that your lender will appreciate getting the full story more than anything else.

Since you (hopefully) started with a high level of transparency when evaluating potential lending partners, give each firm a chance to demonstrate how they respond to that information. Then, before making a much longer-term commitment, you get to decide on the right firm to partner with your business.

BE PROACTIVE

Beyond sharing the full picture of the current state of the business, don't wait to communicate good or bad news. Lenders have to spend a lot of their time chasing down founders and companies trying to get the latest update on the business, the most recent monthly financing reporting, status of ongoing equity fundraise discussions, or all of the above. Do your best to be up front with key updates about the business.

Set up a quarterly meeting with your lender to cover the state of the business and answer any questions they have or perhaps meeting on the same cadence of your normal board discussions. Review the board deck and debrief the lender on the board discussion that followed. Keep that meeting on the calendar even when updates are light. If something significant happens between meetings, proactively share it.

Build a casual texting level of relationship with the top one or two people at your lending partner and treat them like any other board member or observer; this will put your business above all the other portfolio companies who are generally reactive. It will also, oddly enough, free up time in the long run. The lender will see a portfolio company that is not only being very transparent but also is proactive in sharing any meaningful updates, creating a significant amount of trust. Trust is the currency that underpins the bulk of all lender's decisions. If they trust you, they will spend their time chasing down portfolio companies with whom they don't have a close relationship, allowing you to focus on running the actual business.

BE DIRECT

Sharing the positive and the negative is synonymous with being direct, but they are not exactly the same thing. Relationship-building comes from spending time getting to know each other, but it also benefits from quickly getting to the core of an issue. Do your best not to sugarcoat the negative or exaggerate the positive. Giving your lender the gritty, unvarnished state of the business will result in their real reaction sooner and speed up the feedback cycle for any changes that might need to be made to the lending agreement. You can also empower your lending partner to do the same; ask them to give you regular, direct feedback on how they feel about the riskiness of the debt they have provided the company.

AVOID SURPRISES IF POSSIBLE

It is usually a very bad day when a venture lender has to update internal decision-makers at their firm about a portfolio company that has, without warning, lost two of their biggest customers, missed their plan significantly, or the new lead investor on their next equity round has walked, etc. It's bad because it means the debt now carries more inherent risk than before and the decision-makers within the bank or private credit fund will question whether their relationship team actually knows what is going on and, by extension, whether the company is sharing the latest updates in a timely manner.

We've already talked about the need to proactively share both the good and the bad. To add some further nuance related to surprises, if you think there are a range of outcomes for any given situation, share those with your lender. A large new contract, an equity fundraise, possibility of churn in the customer, the list goes on. I'd suggest sharing what you think is the most likely outcome for any of those scenarios but also highlight other potential outcomes, particularly ones that would have a significant negative impact, even if it's a low possibility. That might feel like overkill, but again, it will give your lender much more confidence in your collective understanding of the business and ability to scenario plan as needed. A lender doesn't expect minute levels of detail for every single line item in the business, but for any material outcome or decision, have a Plan A, Plan B, and Plan C in mind.

If you are sharing the good/bad and you're thinking about various scenarios and communicating proactively, the odds of surprising your lender are relatively low. Of course, not everything can be predicted and there can truly be last-minute surprises for a company that catch everyone off guard. Lenders understand that possibility and won't knock a portfolio company who is truly dealing with something in real time. What they will measure a company on is how quickly the executive team communicated the problem to the board and the lender, so the collective group can work together on next steps. If you have any inkling that a change in the business would be surprising to your lending partner, call the senior member of your lending team to give them a quick heads-up. The founders and CFOs where I have built the strongest relationships over the years all have my mobile number, I have theirs, and we aren't afraid to use them. I've received many a phone call or text message late in the evening or on the weekend when something was not going well. That doesn't bother me at all; I much prefer taking a call or text at an inconvenient time than being surprised after the fact or once it is too late.

UNDER-PROMISE AND OVER-DELIVER

Over my twenty-plus years as a venture lender, I regularly joked with founders that lenders were a lot like Yosemite Sam in *Looney Tunes*; we tended to run around with a dark cloud over our head all the time, constantly thinking about risk and the potential downside of any given scenario. It doesn't mean that lenders are all pessimists—in fact, quite the opposite—but, a lender's primary job is to ensure that debt is fully repaid over time. So, risk management is always top of mind and lenders are looking for any kind of indicator, large or small, that indicates whether risk is increasing or decreasing with a given company or venture debt loan. When a lender and portfolio company start to work together, lenders closely watch to see if the company is going to do what they say they are going to do; this happens less frequently than you might think.

The phrase "under-promise and over-deliver" is one that is used across the business landscape and I don't think I need to explain why it is a good practice. In the context of venture lending, this does not mean that a company can't have audacious goals and share them with their lending partner since this is part of getting any capital provider excited about the business. We've already discussed that the one thing you can say with certainty about a company's forecast is that it is wrong. It's just a question of which direction. Lenders don't hold this against their portfolio companies but will, however, start to care if a company is always missing the expectations *they* set for themselves. Milestones not being met may include new contracts or customer conversion slipping past expected close dates, a product launch being delayed a second time, or investor meetings supposedly going well, then they all start to fizzle. Two companies could end up in the exact same place, but lenders would view the one that set overly rosy expectations that they subsequently missed as the riskier situation.

Wherever possible, you want to set expectations that you are confident you can achieve, even if the actual level of performance you are guiding to isn't wildly impressive. The ability to meet expectations and sometimes exceed them matters more to lenders. The best borrowers tend to gauge the odds in their business surprisingly well, which means they set milestones that are pragmatic and/or realistic.

An entrepreneur and company will get most of the juice out of a lending relationship if they are proactive, keep their lender informed, have built relationships with multiple members of their lending team, and of course, under-promise and over-deliver. Building up a nice reservoir of trust will pay dividends when the company needs that extra bit of flexibility or help from their lending partner.

PUT YOUR LENDER TO WORK IN UNIQUE WAYS

Everything in this chapter so far has been recommendations for what a company, founder, or CFO can do to build a robust working relationship with their lending partner. Done well, that helps a company get more flexibility from their lender when needed. The following list of ideas are ways that a company can put their lender to work for their benefit, beyond the debt they have already provided. Over the years, I offered up a number of these items to my portfolio companies when appropriate. Smart founders took me up on a number of these items regularly, and in a few cases, founders were the ones who originally asked me to help in a unique way that I then co-opted and offered to the rest of my portfolio companies because it was equally useful for all of them.

Ask your lender to vet your equity fundraising pipeline. Lenders aren't the right path to intro you get to new investors except in rare cases. Why? Ask any VC what the best way or channel is to find a new portfolio company and they will all say the same thing: A direct intro from a founder they have already backed. Second to that would be a direct intro from another VC they trust about a promising company. It's a pretty steep drop after that; intros from venture lenders are nowhere near the top of the list. Have I helped a company find a new investor or two? Yes, but it was rare.

What I have done for a number of companies when they were raising more equity is help them decipher which venture capital firms on their target list actually had money to put to work. Venture capital firms that aren't doing great take a long time to die. Fund cycles run twelve to fifteen years or longer now. Most VCs continue to take meetings with new companies to keep optionality open even if they don't have meaningful available capital in their fund to invest. This issue was very pronounced in 2010–2011 as the effects of the 2008 financial crisis were hampering new LP commitments to venture funds. Then it went away for more than a decade until rearing its head again starting in 2024. In the current market, venture capital firms are having a significantly harder time raising new funds on balance, barring a few outliers. As a founder or finance team, you may be able save significant time in your equity fundraising process by sharing your target list with your lender. Ask them to flag anyone they know doesn't have meaningful capital to currently deploy, then move those firms to the bottom tier of your target list or off it entirely.

Get references on any service provider in the ecosystem. The senior members of any venture bank or private credit fund know all the other service providers in the industry. I would regularly trade notes with HR providers, law firms, commercial real estate firms, consulting finance firms, recruiters, etc. If you have a specific pain point and are looking for references or recommendations, your lender is a great resource.

What are other portfolio companies like yours doing to solve this particular problem? Even the smallest venture-lending firms have dozens of portfolio companies and the largest players will have thousands. Knowing what other companies of a similar size and trajectory are doing can be very helpful. Equip your lender with the issue or question you are facing, ask them to informally poll companies they talk to over the next few months, then get the debrief.

Give your lender a topic of interest that is relevant to your company, or better yet, your customers, then help build a dinner series on that topic. I attended or hosted a private dinner at least once a month during my time at SVB, usually filled with ten to fifteen CEOs or CFOs with a group discussion on a particular subject. My team was on a similar cadence. We did this to help our portfolio CEOs and CFOs network with other folks navigating similar problems. It helped us elevate from purely a capital provider to a more meaningful partner. It also was great for business development as we would always invite a few prospects to these dinners. The quality of the other attendees and conversation helped win more business than any other thing my team could do. The best lenders host such curated dinners regularly.

You can help shape these dinners to your benefit. Proactively tell your relationship team what types of companies or topics you have an interest in and perhaps even help source a few interesting people in your own network to join the group, lowering the pressure on the lender to fill every seat. Likely, they will still be happy to foot the bill and you get the benefit of a tailor-made group and/or discussion worth your time.

Find out whether a member of your lending relationship team shares a personal passion of yours, then host events together. I enjoy skiing. I grew up skiing at Squaw Valley (now Palisades) and love spending much of winter there. As I became a more senior member of the

SVB team, I was able to pair that passion with my day job. For years, I co-hosted the SVB Ski House in North Lake Tahoe, where we would bring CEOs, CFOs, and VCs together to ski with guides at Palisades and share a private meal in the evening. More recently, I was hosting single-day snowcat trips in North Lake Tahoe with similar groups.

Aside from being a good excuse to get my employer to subsidize my skiing habit, it was great for relationship-building with my portfolio companies and other people in the innovation ecosystem. Over time, it nicely led to a bunch of new business for SVB. If you enjoy doing something outside of work, chances are relatively high that someone at your lender shares that passion. Be vocal about those hobbies and you might be able to get your lender to subsidize it if it allows them to bring together a small group of similar types of founders or execs. Like private dinners, these kinds of events can result in great business development and relationship-building for lenders. More importantly, I've seen a number of new partnerships, a new lead investor, or new customers come out of group events built around a shared passion.

Share the top three things that can help the company right now. There is a lot of online lamenting by VCs about the lack of regular updates from portfolio companies. If you are a founder or CEO, sending at least a monthly update to your investors would put you in the top 10% of companies. This isn't just good investor relations; it has the potential to help companies solve problems—particularly if you put together a list of the top two or three things you need help with. Finding a high-level contact inside a large potential customer, sourcing good candidates for the VP of marketing opening, looking for mentors for junior execs within your company that you want to level up, etc., are examples of items that your investor base might be able to help with if they know they are a concern.

How do you further increase the potential that people in your network can help with these issues? Include your lender(s) on the same update emails or just truncate it to the list of things where you need help. Active lenders talk with all kinds of people and companies in the innovation ecosystem, similar to investors. Once they are aware of your priorities, you'd be surprised what they may be able to surface to your benefit.

CASE STUDY

A COMPANY WITH NINE LIVES—CLEARCO

This case study is about a fintech company that is an alternative lender. There is a lot of complexity in how this kind of business is structured (numerous legal entities, jurisdictions, etc.) and capitalized (variety of types of equity/debt providers involved) that is made even more confusing by the fact that the business is also itself advancing capital to other companies. I've tried my best to simplify this into a story that is digestible while including enough detail to help show how bonkers this situation became.

Clearco was one the earlier entrants in the modern wave of alternative lenders, following in the footsteps of companies like OnDeck and Kabbage in providing capital to small and medium-sized businesses. In Clearco's case, it was focused on providing non-dilutive working capital financing for e-commerce and SaaS-based businesses. Its average customer had not raised venture capital dollars and was not a perfect fit for most traditional commercial lenders. The Toronto-based company was founded in 2015 by Michele Romanow, Andrew D'Souza, Ivan Gritsiniak, Charlie Feng, and Tanay Delima.

Clearco built a platform that ingested tons of information from potential e-commerce and SaaS customers about its underlying businesses. Clearco could then select the top performers, size and price the capital they provided appropriately, and track ongoing performance, all via a digital interface. Repayment of its revenue-based financing came when its underlying portfolio companies were paid by their customers. Clearco's revenue-based finance product was a new application of a brick-and-mortar financing product that individual retail stores have offered for decades. The company called its revenue-based financing merchant cash advances or MCAs. On average, MCAs were under $100K and their tenure or duration was generally under one year.

The activity between 2015 and 2021 perfectly capture the go-go years of the last innovation economy bull market, with 2021 being the zenith. Clearco's corporate history tracks the broader market almost perfectly. It raised a $70M Series A financing in 2018, led by Emergence Capital and Social Capital, as its business was really beginning to ramp. It deployed $100M to more than 500 companies that year. Less than a year later in mid-2019, Clearco raised a $50M Series B led by Highland Capital. It also brought on its first sizable, $250M asset-based financing ("ABF") vehicle, provided by Arcadia and Upper90.

HOW ALTERNATIVE LENDERS FUND THEIR BUSINESSES

Unlike banks, alternative lenders don't have deposits as a source of funds for their lending activities. Unlike private credit funds, they also typically don't raise pools of capital from LPs that they then invest or lend out. Alternative lenders usually start out funding capital to customers or borrowers from their own balance sheet. In the case of Clearco, those initial dollars came from the venture capital dollars they had raised. That is an expensive form of capital. Some alternative lenders will then put a piece of venture debt in place, very much in line with what is talked about in this book and use that capital to fund some of their lending. Ideally, alternative lenders graduate to a size and predictability of customer funding (also known as originations) where a larger ABF allows them to originate their own lending at scale.

ABF structures are mostly provided by specialty private credit or private equity firms and commercial banks, including SVB. They are complex and time-consuming to put in place, which is why, outside of this case study, we won't be covering them in depth in this book. ABF structures usually take the form of a line of credit; the alternative lender can borrow up and down as needed assuming they have availability. Availability to borrow on the line of credit is driven by a borrowing formula or advance rate against the assets. Assets, in this situation, are a pool of loans or capital advances that the alternative lender has originated to its customers. That pool of assets is typically segregated from the parent company (in this case, Clearco) and moved into a bankruptcy-remote special purpose vehicle ("SPV"). The separate SPV is created specifically for the ABF provider so that if the parent company (in this case, Clearco) were to go out of business, the ABF provider could still be repaid by the underlying customers of the now-shuttered alternative lender. This is what bankruptcy-remote means in this context.

These ABF structures can rapidly scale, providing hundreds of millions of dollars to alternative lenders assuming they are originating high-quality underlying assets. Advance rates can range from 50%–100%, with an advance rate of 80%–90% being pretty common. This means that even the best alternative lenders or originators are funding some portion of the assets they generate with their own cash—a key concept as you read on through this case study.

The goal for alternative lenders is to finance their business in what is called the securitization market, where large banks come in, evaluate the pool of underlying assets/ loans, help with obtaining an external credit rating (from rating agencies such as Moody's S&P, Fitch, etc.), then that pool of loans or capital advances can be sold to fixed-income investors across the globe. This type of financing can provide near-infinite scale and is the least costly form of financing for this industry. Hopefully, all this is slightly clearer than mud.

In early 2021, Clearco closed a $100M Series C financing that was led by Oak HC/FT. The company also closed on a new $250M ABF facility with Credigy. At the time of the combined equity and debt raise, Clearco had originated $2B of working capital advances to more than 4,500 companies. They also rebranded from their original name of Clearbanc to Clearco, partly driven by a desire to level up beyond just the capital they provided, but also to avoid confusion by customers and regulators who may have thought they were an actual bank.

The market opportunity for Clearco was and continues to be sizable. Small businesses have always had trouble accessing meaningful working capital financing. Banks tend to have a hard time figuring out what businesses are creditworthy and which are not, particularly when they are small. E-commerce businesses have had a particularly tough time in getting banks to feel comfortable lending them money unless the business has hit substantial scale ($10M or more in revenues). Banks also tend to have a minimum threshold ($250K, for example) of how much a customer needs to borrow to make it worthwhile to spend the time and cover fixed costs to put the debt in place. And no one would ever accuse banks of being fast movers; new loans with a bank tend to be time-consuming exercises. This is all a way of saying that demand for the capital that Clearco provides was never really an issue. In fact, SVB actually had a partnership with Clearco in 2020. At the time, almost all SVB's lending was to companies that had raised meaningful venture capital dollars but would still be the bank for companies that aspired to raise venture capital. When the latter group asked about potentially borrowing money, SVB would send the e-commerce businesses in that group to Clearco.

That customer demand meant that as Clearco headed toward the end of 2021, it faced a variety of challenges in scaling its business: Managing risk by picking the right customers to fund. Building a capital markets back-end to finance the growing customer base. Scaling the entire team rapidly. Then, out of nowhere, Softbank came calling. Less than six months after the close of the last equity financing, Softbank led a $215M Series D investment into Clearco at north of a $2B post-money valuation.

My team at SVB Canada had been talking to Clearco on and off across 2021 about potential debt financing. Not ABF financing. This capital would be used by Clearco's parent company. The discussions got serious on the heels of the Softbank financing. Clearco was arguably one of the top venture-backed companies in Canada at the time and very well known, given Michele Romanow's prominent role on *Dragon's Den*, Canada's equivalent of *Shark Tank*. The team at Clearco asked SVB to help finance two things: a $40M line of credit that would help further bolster its balance sheet, and a $40M venture debt facility, the proceeds of which could be used to fund some lending experiments with new types of customers. The venture debt could also be used to fund the portion of each MCA that was not already financed by the company's ABF providers. For example, if the ABF provided a 90% advance rate, the company could use the venture debt from SVB to fund the other 10%.

With the recent equity raise, impressive list of investors involved, growing customer base, annual revenues north of $100M, and the value to SVB Canada to bring on such a high-profile business, we were comfortable with its debt request, providing a combined $80M financing proposal in late 2021. This was a competitive process; other lenders were interested in the business as well. Some decent back-and-forth with the company, but SVB Canada ultimately carried the day. Given how this story ends, you can insert *Monty Python's* "and there was much rejoicing" here.

Getting our financing package approved and the legal documents finalized took some time. If you haven't figured it out yet, the corporate structure of alternative lenders is complex. We also needed to make sure we had our arms around the flow of funds through the business; what normal course operations were for Clearco and what we needed to approve explicitly. There were also two big executive departures during this time, Curt Sigfstead (CFO), departed for a new opportunity while Andrew D'Souza (CEO and co-founder) transitioned out of a full-time role to executive chair of the board with Michele Romanow (co-founder) taking over as the new CEO.

In hindsight, perhaps we should have read a little bit more into the state of the business from these transitions, but at the time, the company and board had good rationale for the moves, so we continued moving forward. Our financing for Clearco ultimately closed at the end of Q1 2022—basically, the exact high point of the tech bull market of the prior decade. The company borrowed the entire $80M shortly thereafter. Life was good . . . for a very short time.

After closing the transaction, we started monitoring the company's performance on a regular cadence like we would any other borrower. Clearco continued to see off-the-charts demand from its customers and were originating MCAs at a breakneck pace. It was also growing the team to a high point of more than 500 full-time employees. The growth in headcount was driving operating expenses up, ahead of revenues, and increasing the company's already sizable cash burn. Further affecting cash levels was the timing gap between Clearco providing capital to customers and getting the bulk of that cash back via its ABF financing partners. With its growth and assuming the underlying credit quality of its lending was still within acceptable levels, we weren't worried (yet) about the decreasing cash levels. We also thought the company would still be able to raise equity dollars if or when needed. Both of those assumptions would soon prove faulty.

In July 2022, Clearco's finance team asked, unprompted, for an in-person meeting. Out of left field, they let us know the company was unlikely to make payroll at the end of the week. This was wild news to SVB. We didn't understand how they could be running out of cash given what we thought we knew about the state of the business. The main cause of the issue was a deterioration in the quality of the originations Clearco was providing its customers. Increasing overall tenor or length of time each customer had to repay, delinquencies going up, and more outright losses in the portfolio were materially impacting how much capital Clearco was able to borrow from its ABF providers. The company historically had been able to borrow 85%–90% of the value of MCAs from its ABF providers. Now, the advance rate had decreased to almost 70%, meaning for every new MCA originated, Clearco needed to use 2×–3× its own cash to fund that customer. This had gone on for weeks before the company realized the magnitude of the issue. As interest rates were increasing, the underlying unit economics of the business had also started to erode, and the company had not been fast enough in adjusting pricing.

We at SVB hadn't seen this coming for two primary reasons. All lenders require borrowers to send in their monthly financials thirty days after month-end, which means a thirty-day lag in seeing a company's performance—and most borrowers are chronically late sending in financial reports. As a result, cash had depleted substantially over the prior forty-five days before we saw the monthly financials that would have flagged the issue. On top of that, we were not regularly reviewing entity-level financials, only consolidated financials. The consolidated numbers masked a lot of the credit quality issues across the various SPVs Clearco had in place. This was a big mistake and one we learned the hard way.

Clearco's cash levels were now well below the $80M provided by SVB and close to hitting the cash covenant we had in place for the $40M line of credit, supposedly the less risky portion of SVB's debt package. It required the company to keep $30M of cash at SVB at all times. The company asked for the meeting to give us the real-time update on the business and to ask us to remove the minimum cash threshold, effectively letting them access another $30M that currently was in SVB bank accounts and not at risk. This would allow Clearco to make payroll and continue funding some level of MCAs without interruption.

Where were the board and the rest of the investor syndicate in all this? Good question. They were also caught off guard by the runoff in cash and were scrambling to put together a small equity financing to help capitalize the business. Complicating their desire to fund the business was the fact that the broader landscape of fintech companies, both public and private, was also starting to deteriorate; public fintech valuations had dropped from their highs in late 2021. Affirm and Lending Club, two publicly traded lenders at the time, saw their market caps drop by 68% and 90% respectively, from their high-water marks in 2021 to their low points of 2022. You can imagine the impact that kind of valuation reset in the public markets was having on private market fundraising.

The majority of investors were supportive of putting in more cash, but they couldn't get it done in two days to help the company avoid missing payroll. The Clearco team was asking us to allow the $30M sitting at SVB to be used to fill that gap, then agree to bring cash back to that level within sixty days. In that time frame, it could close the new equity financing and sort out the issues with its ABF providers. SVB has prided itself on being the most patient lender in the venture-lending ecosystem, willing to work hard with borrowers to find the right path forward, in good and bad times. We deliberated internally and ultimately decided we would allow the company to dip below the minimum cash threshold and access the $30M sitting at SVB. For our flexibility, we required the company to close the new bridge equity in short order, engage an investment bank to run an M&A process (something it was going to do anyway) and to have $30M of cash back at SVB within sixty days.

You may be asking why we were flexible in this situation when we weren't in the Phone Tap situation. The main difference is the continued support and investment from the board, which wasn't the case with Phone Tap.

The board also brought in an external adviser, Andrew Curtis, to help figure out the right capital markets and lending mix for the company. Andrew had spent significant time in private equity, leverage finance, and the asset-based finance industry over his career. While he didn't have any direct start-up experience, his understanding of most types of lending, underwriting, risk management, and unit economics quickly became critical to the business. He also had a keen awareness of how to build productive relationships with lenders, something that would pay dividends down the road.

Clearco made it through its early summer payroll issue and funded a new $20M investor bridge financing shortly after SVB relaxed the minimum cash covenant. Unfortunately, that didn't resolve the broader headwinds impacting the whole of the fintech world or the funding issues that the company was having with its ABF providers.

To save you a bit of time, I'm going to summarize the next six months with Clearco in one paragraph: We had weekly calls with the company to understand the state of the business and its work resolving capital markets issues and bi-weekly calls with investors and the investment bank running the M&A process. Initially, we thought there would be at least some interest to acquire the business but a price well below the last post-money valuation. That hope quickly dwindled with the broader market issues and, by end of 2022, had all but disappeared with no viable acquisition options. SVB brought in a restructuring firm to help diligence the state of the business and advise the bank on possible next steps.

Clearco worked hard trying to get its ABF providers comfortable but didn't succeed. Those providers turned off new originations and started to amortize their facilities with Clearco; they were getting their loans paid down as Clearco's customers repaid their MCAs, but Clearco was no longer able to originate new capital advances. This meant what was formerly a $100M revenue business had been reduced to near zero. The company did multiple layoffs over this time period and ultimately saw Michele Romanow step down as CEO to be replaced by Andrew Curtis, the right move given the focus was no longer on growth but survival. A small subset of existing investors led by Inovia (Karam Nijjar) were working to put together a full equity recap of the business; it clearly wasn't worth anywhere near the $2B valuation of its last fundraise in 2021. Further, when you have a business that is barely generating revenue, has in-flux underlying unit economics, and is evaluating an equip recap, $80M of outstanding debt (from SVB) becomes a glaring problem. Way too much debt given the state of the business.

The conversations I was having with Andrew, Karam at Inovia, the ABF lenders, and our restructuring firm had shifted primarily toward how to restructure the SVB debt to allow the business to continue to operate, or alternatively, whether the business should just shut down or be sold for salvage value. We were all trying to keep the business alive but were also understandably pragmatic about the various paths forward. At this point, I thought it very likely the company was headed toward bankruptcy and SVB toward a sizable loan loss. There were no easy answers or paths forward in early March 2023 when suddenly, SVB failed.

You've already read the SVB Case Study, so I won't belabor it here other than to say I'm glad I survived a bank failure on two sides of an international border but really don't ever want to do that again.

Andrew and I had become close over the past year given how much work we were doing to keep the business alive. Once we both got over the shock of SVB's failure, we initially thought this was also very bad news for Clearco. With the size of the debt SVB provided to Clearco, decisions that needed to be made about restructuring or possibly even charging off (SVB taking a loss) some or all of the debt would have needed to go up to the executive levels of the bank. Now, it was unclear who those decision-makers were.

SVB Canada was the primary lender to Clearco, but a small portion of the debt was actually held by SVB Capital. We often shared a portion of larger venture debt structures with our SVB Capital team (you may recall they are now a stand-alone entity named Pinegrove Capital Partners). SVB Canada was a foreign branch of SVBFG, the publicly traded entity in the US that was now in bankruptcy. SVB Capital, as a part of SVBFG, was also in a state of purgatory. Canada's Office of the Superintendent of Financial Institutions (OSFI) took over SVB Canada the weekend of SVBFG's failure. Then PWC's restructuring team took over operations of SVB Canada, via court appointment, to facilitate a bankruptcy sale process. At the time, it was completely unclear how we would make the necessary changes to help Clearco survive, let alone get the SVB debt repaid. But Andrew and I agreed to keep talking daily. Before signing off on the weekend the bank failed, we chuckled at how ironic it was that SVB had failed since we both thought Clearco had been much closer to death's door. Gallows humor.

The PWC restructuring team was on-site at SVB Canada's main office in Toronto that weekend to begin getting their arms around the business. SVB's Canada branch was only licensed to lend to Canadian companies, so thankfully did not have any deposits (or lack thereof) to worry about. It had a sizable loan portfolio of borrowers who were understandably worried about their ability to continue to access capital. Clearco was the largest borrower in the Canadian portfolio at the time of SVB's failure. PWC went through the entire list of borrowers, wanting to understand each borrower's business, the risk profile, whether each company might need or want to draw down additional capital, etc.

It was important to understand the state of the portfolio because PWC really had two options for SVB Canada. One was to let the portfolio pay back naturally over time, then to shut down the branch. The second option was to facilitate a sale of the loan portfolio or the whole of SVB Canada to the highest bidder. This was the start of building a database to use during a potential sale process that was to come. Because of the way a bankruptcy sale process works in Canada and many other countries, it was likely to take six to nine months to get to a final buyer. There were a variety of formal checkpoints with the bankruptcy judge, plus court-mandated time frames to allow public review of potential bids to purchase the portfolio. This was quickly going to become a very not fun purgatory for SVB Canada's portfolio companies and employees.

Our best companies would likely find other lenders to refinance their existing debt while the borrowers that were low on liquidity or not performing would be stuck waiting for the sale process to conclude, all while not knowing how PWC would make decisions. Amid many conversations with PWC, my team and I gave them the state of play with Clearco and quickly advocated that they should run a separate sale process for the Clearco debt; otherwise, it was highly likely the company would fail. Clearco wouldn't be able to raise more equity or convince its ABF lenders to be flexible if the SVB debt to the parent company was sitting in purgatory.

If it wasn't clear already, I am American. I was officially the token, best, and only American involved with SVB Canada. That means I had to learn on the fly where business or legal norms differed between the US and Canada. Quebec, as a province in Canada, for example, operates almost like a wholly separate country within greater Canada: different language (French), different legal foundation (civil law vs.

common law in the rest of Canada), different business customs, etc. A more relevant Canadian difference for this story is that federal law in Canada allows a bankruptcy judge and court-appointed monitor (PWC) to consider a broader set of stakeholders when making decisions. They want to appease creditors and maximize the sale of assets, but ongoing employment and operational continuity of the underlying companies could be factors considered as well.

After several weeks of ongoing dialogue between my team, Clearco, and members of the board, PWC and the bankruptcy judge thankfully agreed to run a separate sale process for just the Clearco debt to help keep the company alive and, by extension, keep a couple hundred Canadians employed. A subset of the existing investors led by Inovia and joined by SVB Capital (navigating their own sale process in the US) plus Founder's Circle Capital cobbled together a bid to purchase the $60M of debt to Clearco held by SVB Canada. The smaller $20M portion held by SVB Capital (now Pinegrove) would stay in place.

It took a few more weeks to allow other offers to come in but ultimately, the Inovia-led bid was approved. The purchase price was well below par value given the state of Clearco's business and lack of other meaningful bids. Upon completion of the sale, the investors equitized the debt (converted the debt into equity, part of their plan all along) and then promptly funded new equity into the business. SVB Capital, which held the remaining $20M note to Clearco, would be the only debt remaining to the parent company. After all that cleanup, Clearco's ABF providers were willing to renegotiate their own agreements and start lending again to the company. Life was, amazingly, kind of back to normal.

AFTERMATH

Fast-forward to present day and Clearco is still operating as this book goes to print. Having faced multiple rounds of layoffs, an equity recap, its primary bank and lender failing, a subset of the investors successfully purchasing the SVB Canada debt out of bankruptcy, then equitizing that debt and restructuring the ABF facilities multiple times over. Any one of those things would be enough to kill a company. To say Andrew Curtis and the Clearco team have a high tolerance for pain and have also done impressive work would be an understatement.

You might think that a lot of us at SVB, me included, had other things on our minds during the bank failure and subsequent sale process. While true and even though our day jobs were very much in question, we wanted to make sure that our failure didn't kill Clearco or any other portfolio company, for that matter. There was a moment there, given how interconnected and central SVB was to the ecosystem, that we thought every venture-backed company could be at risk because of SVB's failure. Thankfully, that worst-case scenario didn't come to pass.

KEY TAKEAWAYS

Over-leveraging is one of the key risks to a company when taking on venture debt. This issue is even more pronounced when talking about debt to an alternative lender. At SVB, we learned a number of lessons with Clearco that, in hindsight, perhaps should have been obvious. Lending large dollars to the parent company of an alternative lender is not a good idea. If the business is operating well, it is selling all the assets or capital advances it generates to their ABF providers. That means that even in the best cases, alternative lenders will have minimal assets on their balance sheet other than their own cash. In our defense, we originally had a minimum cash requirement governing part of the SVB debt, and based on conversations with the company, expected some amount of its MCA origination to stay on its balance sheet. Neither of those things were true in the end. Further, the revenue and growth in any alternative lending business model assumes ongoing origination. If that same alternative lender gets sideways with its ABF provider(s) and doesn't have its own cash to continue origination themselves . . . the business essentially drops to zero. Quickly.

Everyone (company, board, SVB) should have been paying more attention to the specifics of each ABF structure, plus the ongoing health of
the relationship between the company and the ABF teams.

**More equity raised at higher and higher valuations is not always
a good thing.** Clearco is one of the poster children for the potential
downsides of raising too much money too quickly. Given the market at
the time, the company was understandably focused on growth at close
to all costs which was being rewarded heavily in 2019–2021. Money
was falling out of trees and hitting people on the head. Everyone in
the innovation economy was doing this. The downside is that a lot of
the "unicorns" minted in 2020 and 2021 will likely not survive in their
current form. The amount of equity raised and the valuation high
point that Clearco hit in 2021 arguably made it much more painful
to reset the equity stack and raise a small round to keep the business
afloat after it hit massive headwinds.

As this book goes to print, venture capital is pouring into any
company that has an AI product and a pulse. Valuation levels are sky-
rocketing and regularly being referenced in funding round announcements as a proxy for the current state of the business. Will there be
some lifechanging AI businesses that stand the test of time? Definitely.
Will there also be a lot of pain to come with companies that don't
achieve the ever-increasing expectations? Most definitely. It's something to keep in mind when deciding how to capitalize your own business or which start-up you might want to join.

**Picking the right venture debt provider and building a solid
working relationship with them will pay dividends, in good and bad
times.** We built a solid relationship with everyone at Clearco, including the founders and original finance team. When Andrew Curtis
was brought on in the middle of 2022, that relationship got even better although weird to say given the state of Clearco's business at the
time. Andrew was quick to start solving for the underlying issues with
Clearco's business model. Equally important, though, he was proactive

and honest with all of the company's partners, SVB in particular. That helped our willingness to provide flexibility when needed and, in the end, to advocate on the company's behalf with PWC to run a separate sale process for Clearco's debt. If you'll forgive my forwardness, Clearco chose its partner well when borrowing money. SVB was willing to be flexible when it was necessary, even in several cases when it was likely to be to SVB's potential detriment. Few firms out there will provide similar flexibility when push comes to shove. It continues to be important to choose wisely.

Sometimes truth is stranger than fiction. Arguably, Clearco should have failed. I've seen any one of the problems the company faced kill other businesses. Bizarrely, had SVB itself not failed, Clearco would likely be dead; I don't see how we (SVB) could have resolved the overhang of the debt we provided to the parent company otherwise. Canadian law allowing for ongoing employment to be considered in bankruptcy was also another stroke of luck and yet another reason beyond hockey and maple syrup to love Canada. The number of things that had to go right for Clearco to survive and continue (re)building its business was staggering. Yet here we are.

11

RED FLAGS THAT
MAKE LENDERS CAUTIOUS

Lenders are always on the lookout for risk(s) coming around the corner and trying to avoid what, in hindsight, might have been an obvious red flag. Most firms have several internal triggers or situations they consider more inherently risky compared to the average start-up. These lessons have most often been learned the hard way with a portfolio company failing and the lender unexpectedly losing money. The most meaningful insights have come when a handful of portfolio companies have experienced distress caused by the same issue. Every part of this chapter describes company profiles or situations that are perceived as higher risk for lenders.

If you find your start-up checks one or more of these boxes, that doesn't mean you are headed toward a bad outcome or that they are deal-breakers for the venture-lending community. However, you should be aware of the perception that lenders will have as they evaluate your business. Ideally, you should do your best to address their concerns up front so they know you are cognizant of the issues. That may or may not be enough to get lenders comfortable to provide capital in the first place or provide flexibility if you've already taken their money, but it will give you a better chance in either case.

LESS THAN 12 MONTHS OF CASH

With a year or less of cash, a venture-backed company is entering the highest-risk time frame start-ups face, where they will have to successfully raise more equity to avoid dying. All venture lenders expect the debt they provide to be used to provide runway extension and so are comfortable lending through these risky time frames. However, they generally want to avoid starting a venture-lending relationship immediately before an equity raise. Seems a little counterintuitive, doesn't it?

The thinking goes like this: A company with less than a year of runway has very likely already started having preliminary conversations with investors (external and insiders) about a new round of equity. If the feedback from the investor community has been resoundingly positive, it is unlikely that a company will seek out a new venture debt facility. Companies that may have talked with investors and received early responses that were less than favorable turn to the debt markets to extend runway. Future equity infusions are one the largest sources of repayment that venture lenders count on, so you can see where the optics of this type of situation become problematic. A secondary issue is the company's inability to see a tough equity fundraise coming (barring crazy macro environment changes) and seek out debt capital earlier. Lenders don't like the lack of foresight. Additionally, a lender hasn't worked with the company for any length of time and achieved the benefit of a good working relationship.

If you find your company facing this situation, hopefully the metrics of the business are decent and your board is actively supportive. You will need their help in convincing lenders that if the debt is put in place and the company can't find an outside lead investor, the existing investor syndicate is willing and capable of stepping up to fund the business. Investor capacity and willingness to continue funding a portfolio company is always a meaningful part of venture-lending diligence, but with less than twelve months of cash, it really becomes THE primary question. When you start talking to lenders, you'll probably lose a few straight away because they'll hear *less than twelve months of cash* and quickly pass. You should consider talking to a larger number of lenders (eight to ten) out of the gate to increase the chances of having a few term sheets at the end of everyone's diligence process.

This red flag is mostly applicable to early- and mid-stage companies. Later-stage companies may seek out a large venture debt facility when lower on liquidity to displace a final equity round before hitting break-even and saving unnecessary dilution for all shareholders. This is usually the case when the business is humming along and the likelihood of raising additional equity, if needed, is very high. Even in these situations, later-stage companies should ideally start a dialogue with lenders before having less than a year of cash to avoid having to rush the venture debt fundraise.

A SOLO LEAD INVESTOR

Having a single main or lead investor is a somewhat counterintuitive red flag because it can be both a positive and a negative. Welcome to a lender's brain. Suppose a company has raised a $15M Series A round with $12M from a well-known fund and the remainder from a long tail of angels and seed investors. On the surface, having a brand-named fund with enough conviction to take that much of the round is a positive indicator. The potential downside that lenders have in the back of their minds is what happens down the road when the company needs to raise a Series B. If everything is going great and the business is knocking it out of the park, equity fundraising won't be an issue. That's true regardless of stage, investor syndicate, or any other red flag. Outstanding company performance trumps almost any other issue.

However, when the company is only doing okay or not hitting expectations, then a single large lead investor can become a potential problem. In that situation, the company may have trouble finding a new outside lead investor and may need support from the existing shareholders on the cap table. Now the single large investor is going to have to (1) come to their own conclusion about continuing to support the business and (2) grapple with just how much money they want to invest into a single portfolio company.

Let's unpack both problems. Investors will talk your ear off about how they think independently, are contrarian, and have a bunch of internal themes they follow, regardless of what others are doing. There are certainly some exceptional firms and partners that consistently and impressively do this. But in my experience, and I hope my friends in the venture community will forgive me for saying this, there is a lot of groupthink and FOMO (fear of missing out) involved in the investing world, especially when the market is on the upswing. For entrepreneurs, that isn't always a bad thing, particularly if you are the recipient of that investor interest.

When one fund is the only significant investor involved and, perhaps, the only outside board member, they're not going to look around the boardroom and say, *Well, it's us and two other well-heeled investors. We've all got deep pockets and can support the business through this tough spot.* Having other people around on the cap table who are supportive can make it easier for them to get to "yes." That social proof can at times be critical. Instead, that fund has to make a call to be supportive, or not, on their own. From my experience, there is a higher chance of the answer being a "no" if things aren't going well. So, a word of caution to all the entrepreneurs out there: even if total dollars invested are the same, more often than not, having a few firms with decent ownership stakes in the business early on is going to be better than one firm wowing you with how much they love the business and being the sole meaningful investor.

Two other minor issues that occasionally rear their head when one firm has taken the majority of an early round are reserves and the internal concentration limits of the fund—how much capital is set aside for follow-on investment in the same company and how much a fund can invest into any single portfolio company. After investing into a new portfolio company, most venture funds reserve further dollars to continue supporting the company over time. Reserve levels will vary based on the size, stage, and philosophy of the venture fund, but something like 1× to 2× initial capital invested would not be uncommon. Internal concentration limits for each fund are set in each fund's formation docs, usually between 10% and 15%. To go above that limit, a fund would need to get explicit LP approval and is something most funds are unlikely to do. In the case of the company that raised $12M of a $15M Series A round from one fund, it becomes possible, even if unlikely, that their main investor may need to think about just how much money they want to deploy into one business, especially if the fund was less than $300M ($12M initial investment + $25M in reserves > 10% of total fund). With the increasing fund sizes of most of the brand-name venture firms, the concentration issue has become less prevalent in the last few years. Whether the rise of mega fund sizes ($1B or more) continues is anyone's guess, but something to watch.

How will lenders approach the single-lead investor situation? It might not affect term sheets if the company looks stellar otherwise. It is possible you might see different terms from lenders who won't be as aggressive or as flexible as requested. You might also see a financial covenant or two in the deal structure depending on the lender's perspective. As with most things, it depends.

THE ORPHANED PORTFOLIO COMPANY

This situation usually sucks for everybody: An orphaned portfolio company is where the partner and board member representing a large fund on the cap table has left the firm, leaving all their portfolio companies "orphaned." Partners leave a venture fund for a variety of reasons; some retire, return to be an operator, aren't very good investors and are asked to leave, or some start their own fund. The list goes on. Unlike the concentration issue, orphaned portfolio companies are more common these days as the headcount turnover within venture funds has increased. The orphaned portfolio companies have lost the person with whom they had the strongest relationship, who knew the business well, and who advocated on their behalf within the venture partnership. Once that partner is gone, the odds are low that the company will get the same level of engagement or conviction from the fund going forward.

In the best cases—and it's rare—a well-known partner in the fund immediately picks up that board seat. That's usually a pretty good indicator that the fund thinks very highly of the company and its potential. More often than not, the new person will be a more junior partner or principal who takes over responsibility for the fund's investment in the company: a less exciting indicator of that firm's view of the company.

In some cases, orphaned companies might not get anyone to take the place of the investor, and a fund might say, *We're not going to fill the board seat*, which is never a good sign. Some funds have operating partners who play cleanup for their orphaned or troubled portfolio companies, and while it's good to have someone from the fund on the board, that person also might have ten or twenty board seats. This isn't a very large vote of confidence from the firm either.

The tough part of being an orphaned company, which is usually no fault of the company itself, is that not only has their champion within the venture fund left, but the new board member doesn't have any skin in the game and will be hard-pressed to become an advocate. If the company performs and becomes a breakout success, the new partner gets the benefit of being the face of the investment even if they didn't source the original deal. If the company meanders along and fails sometime down the road, the new partner can wipe their hands of the outcome because it wasn't "their" investment. So, a lot of potential negative outcomes when a company is orphaned mean the odds of continued investment from that particular fund, everything else being equal, decreases.

All of these things—less than twelve months of runway, a single investor, or being orphaned—will impact how venture lenders view the initial lending opportunity but are also ongoing points of risk across all their portfolio companies. When a portfolio company has less than twelve months of cash, the lender will pay more attention to what's going on in the company than they would otherwise. If the company has one main investor, lenders will pay more attention to the company until the cap table becomes meaningfully diversified. All of these "red flags" have carryover into the ongoing relationship between the lender and the founders or companies that are borrowing the money.

THERE IS NO BOARD

Operating without a board really only happens during a company's earliest stages. We've already discussed that most venture lending happens with companies that have raised at least one sizable institutional round of equity, typically a Series A, or a large "seed" round. Lending to a company that has only raised a small seed round does happen occasionally from a select group of banks and funds, particularly now that the funding landscape for very early-stage companies is so built out. Seed, pre-seed, large seed, micro-VC; each have their own definitions and participants. Round sizes across all stages have generally inflated as well. There are regular funding announcements of $10M to $15M "seed" rounds. Series A companies regularly have products in market, early customers, and decent revenue levels; ten years ago, they would have mostly been pre-product launch or just a presentation about what they hope to build.

To sort through all this noise, venture lenders either stick to only lending to Series A-funded companies that have one or more significant lead investors or, if a particular lender is going to provide capital to a seed-stage company, will commonly want to see at least one outside investor on the board. Companies that don't have a formal board yet can still be filled with great founders and have loads of potential. Lenders only use the outside board member as a proxy for the level of diligence or involvement of investors and the overall level of governance. They want to ensure that investors have enough skin in the game to be motivated to continue to support the company over time. Remember, the primary source of repayment for venture lenders from early-stage companies is proceeds from future equity raises. So, understanding who is on the cap table and their financial capacity and willingness to continue supporting the company is of paramount importance. If a company doesn't have a formal board yet, they are unlikely to get significant lender interest.

DEBT LARGER THAN INVESTMENT FROM THE LARGEST SHAREHOLDER

How "invested" are the founders, employees, and shareholders in the business? Lenders spend a lot of time to decipher exactly that. Skin in the game is a close proxy for how motivated each group will be to slog through days, months, and years of hard work to get to a potentially good outcome. Most diligence centers, like everything else, on the cap table. When lenders evaluate a new company, one of many things they will do early on is see how much capital each of the preferred shareholders has invested in the business, not just purely percentage ownership. This is good info to have for a number of reasons, but one quick check is whether the requested debt amount is less than the largest dollar investor(s). Lenders don't usually like to provide venture debt that is the largest outside check in the business; they prefer to have someone else or multiple parties with more capital committed. I can tell you from experience that in the few cases in my portfolio where the venture debt was the largest outside check AND the company was not performing, odds were much higher that the board would just hand the lender the keys and say *It's your problem now.*

As companies scale to meaningful traction and revenues, call it Series C or greater in equity raised, this issue starts to matter less and less. With more company-specific performance and metrics to evaluate, the importance of investor psychology diminishes. Debt levels will be measured against revenues or ARR. Speaking of which . . .

DEBT GREATER THAN REVENUE

Debt greater than revenue is often applicable to later-stage borrowers who have tens of millions in revenue, ARR, or both. Early-stage companies may not have revenue or be in the early innings of their ramp, so lenders appropriately focus a lot more on investor syndicate. For later-stage companies, lenders normally want to see available debt at or below 1:1 trailing twelve-month revenue or, more commonly, ARR. Depending on the situation, this could be accomplished from appropriately sizing the debt from the start to match revenue or ARR levels, or the available debt may be governed with a borrowing formula or performance milestones that keep it within that 1:1 level. The concern lenders have about going over the 1:1 threshold is the potential to over-leverage the business and debt service becoming too great a portion of operating expenses. This will hamper other parts of the business, and if the company needs to raise equity at any point going forward, new investors may balk at the size and scale of the debt load.

Ideally, don't ask for a debt amount from lenders exceeding that 1:1 level, but if you do, I recommend you be very cautious about actually borrowing up to that threshold. Exceptions to this would be for companies whose growth trajectory is best in class. Debt levels greater than 1:1 may well be justified if revenue growth quickly catches up and allows the business to move faster. Either way, buyer beware.

12

RED FLAGS THAT SHOULD MAKE ENTREPRENEURS CAUTIOUS

Turnabout is fair play. I've shared a few rules of thumb lenders use to quickly evaluate current and future portfolio companies. In this chapter, I share similar areas of caution or "red flags" for entrepreneurs, CFOs, and boards as they evaluate various lending partners. Other than personal guarantees (see next section), none of these should be deal-breakers in and of themselves, but entrepreneurs should make their decision with eyes wide open. Know what type of lender you are starting a relationship with, both their strengths and their weaknesses, before making the final call.

PERSONAL GUARANTEES

In the unlikely event you happen to see a *personal guarantee* requested in a term sheet from a potential lender, your decision is easy. Take said term sheet, put it in the old shredder, thank the lender for their time, then let them know you'll be going with another provider. Personal guarantees haven't been a part of venture-lending transactions for decades, partly because most founders who start a company don't have a lot of financial wherewithal, but primarily because everyone realizes the default outcome in Start-Up Land is failure. So, if a lender is actually asking for a personal guarantee, they are either wildly ignorant of the risk they may be taking, which is bad for everybody, they are potentially being predatory in their lending philosophy, or possibly both. Don't spend much time thinking about this. If you see this in a term sheet, just walk. Life is too short.

NEW ENTRANTS

One of the better measures of a firm is longevity—has the fund or venture bank been doing this for a long time? Do they have a track record of navigating at least one or more business cycles where they consistently provided capital throughout? Having successfully operated through the up and downside of the market cycle in the innovation economy doesn't make a lender perfect but it does, however, signal a few things. It tells you that the lender has already seen a subset of portfolio companies underperform and potentially fail. If you are portfolio company n + 1, you won't be dealing with an institution that is still figuring out lending philosophy, guidelines, etc. Further, the fact that the fund or bank is still active in the ecosystem means that senior leadership in the firm are comfortable with the potential risk involved, having seen it firsthand already. The venture-lending ecosystem has some historically famous new entrants who then exited a few years later after having a change of heart.

Right now, a lender would have to have been in business since 2021 to have seen the innovation market turnover before the AI craze fully kicked in. In 2020, it had been a long time since the down market (2008–2009), so any new entrants between 2010 and 2020 had only experienced the up cycle of business. You can find out when a lender started their practice by looking at their website, reading their 10Q or 10K (if public), consulting your favorite LLM, or just asking the firm directly. Did they get into venture lending last year? Did they start doing it five years ago? Has it been a multi-decade journey? Everything else being equal, being in the business longer is better.

But all new entrants are not created equal. For example, after the collapse of SVB, some talented people left and started fresh with new employers, several of whom had never actively pursued venture lending or had only just started fledgling efforts. In those organizations, you've got really experienced people (formerly at SVB) who have gone through market cycles and have a world-class approach to venture lending, but they are at a new firm that they don't fully control. That doesn't mean they're going to be bad partners, far from it, but it does mean that there is a bit of a question mark about the broader institution's intestinal fortitude for the innovation economy. Banks and private credit funds that have been around for years have a more known reputation. That doesn't mean those lenders all have *good* reputations, but they're known in the market and it's not a question mark about how they operate through cycles.

RENEGOTIATING TERMS

Negotiating heavily before a term sheet is signed is expected. Sometimes the back-and-forth will be protracted and potentially heated; other times, it will be pretty smooth and painless. Regardless of the type of negotiation, once the term sheet has been executed by both parties, the deal points are locked. As legal documents are drafted and reviewed by outside counsel, another round of negotiation kicks off for all the items that weren't fully flushed out in the term sheet or not mentioned at all; we covered a number of those potential hot buttons earlier in the book. All of this is normal and even expected.

What is not normal is that after a term sheet is signed, the lender comes back to try to change the business points of the deal, unprompted. By *unprompted*, I mean there hasn't been some material change in the performance of the business or some new piece of information uncovered. It also means you haven't asked to change other business points and they are just responding in kind.

If truly unprompted, it is time to walk. As painful as it will be to restart a process with other lenders, it is better than allowing a firm to walk back the specifics of a term sheet. If they do that now, imagine what they'll do in the future. Assuming you were cordial with other lenders who had been vying for your business, they will be stoked to hear from you. Trust me, I've been in their shoes. Nothing feels better after having lost a deal and opportunity to work with a great company than to find out your competitor did something immensely stupid and now that company wants to rekindle the conversation.

JUNIOR TEAM MEMBERS

Something we saw at SVB during recent downturns in the innovation economy was how hierarchy or seniority at a venture fund played a significant role in which portfolio companies continued to be supported. You could have a portfolio company with several brand-name venture funds on the cap table, but if the partner involved was relatively new or junior, it could quickly become a problem. When faced with a downturn and a large number of portfolio companies that needed support, venture funds went into triage mode to decide who was deserving of additional capital. If a portfolio company was a clear outlier or winner (a rare situation), they were supported regardless of whose portfolio company it was. For companies that weren't a clear outlier, one of the biggest predictors we found of ongoing support (i.e., more equity dollars) was the seniority of the partner involved. If the partner's name was on the door or they helped build the firm (and even if the company wasn't great), it would still get additional capital from the firm. If you were a junior partner, a recent hire, or a venture partner, odds were not good that you'd be able to win the battle of wits at the partnership meeting on Monday morning.

For venture firms, the forcing function that caused this squeeze was the finite amount of capital that each fund raises and, over time, the amount of capital left to support remaining portfolio companies. Also, the fact that venture firms typically can't cross-pollinate or invest into the same company from multiple funds is a factor, at least not without significant headache. Private credit funds can sometimes face similar issues around a limited pool of capital to support companies. Banks don't generally have issues with capital available to support existing or potential portfolio companies. However, the importance of seniority remains, mostly driven by track record and trust. Tenured members of a tech bank or private credit fund have many reps underwriting and getting approval for new venture debt. The internal investment or credit committee members have likely seen these lenders handle a large portfolio, including a variety of challenging situations. Just like lenders are evaluating how companies perform and do what they say they are going to do, lenders are held to the same standard within their own firm. Is a lender able to predict what their portfolio companies are going to do or need? Are they able to get to the right outcome for both the lender and company, even if it involves some hard conversations? The more senior lenders build up the subsequent scar tissue, skill set, and trust of their internal partners, the more leeway they'll have with their portfolio companies and the faster they'll move when deals need to get done.

More senior lenders can also be beneficial to a company in seeing potential problems around the corner and being willing to have candid dialogue early. I've been on both sides of this coin in my career. As a junior team member managing a portfolio of companies, I might not be able to anticipate concerns my firm might have with a specific business. Earlier in my career, it was a much larger effort to flag an issue I had seen to a founder, CFO, or exec team. That takes high levels of self-awareness, business acumen, and communication skills that your average junior lender, including me back in the day, don't generally have in their tool kit. Later in my career, I did all that regularly and built better relationships with my portfolio companies. I also had more internal credibility with senior credit officers, which allowed me to move faster and win more business with great companies, even if at the edge of our comfort zone.

There will always be a mix of seniority levels across lenders you engage with. If you end up dealing with somebody who is more junior or early in their career, that's not necessarily bad, but the odds will be lower that they have the institutional weight to argue for something unique or creative on your behalf when you need it. The upside of a good junior member of a lending team is they tend to be uber responsive. This drives home the point that you should build multiple relationships and touchpoints with your capital provider. When I was a junior relationship manager, I would regularly bring out the managing director of my team, a good friend to this day, who helped bring credibility to the conversation and took point on several founder or CEO relationships. If your lender doesn't offer the chance to meet additional—and ideally, more senior—members of the team, ask for it. They will likely be happy to oblige.

13

THE POTENTIAL DOWNSIDES
OF VENTURE DEBT

I've done my best to be evenhanded throughout the pages of this book and give you both sides of any argument. I spent most of my career at SVB, a bank, but I've striven to give you the pros and cons of working with both banks AND private credit funds. What I haven't covered in the book are the potential downsides of taking on venture debt at all. Just like venture capital investment, there are situations where too much or any venture debt can be problematic. Sometimes, venture debt has definitely been the cause of a company's demise, though thankfully, pretty rare. However, it has happened enough over the years that a few prominent investors and funds are pretty vocal in their dislike of venture debt. For example:

Paul Graham ✔   **X**
@paulg · **Follow**

Venture debt is like a delicious sandwich that only costs ten cents, but occasionally explodes in your face.

If I were running a startup, I don't think I'd ever take it.

2:53 AM · Feb 7, 2020   ⓘ

❤ **1.1K**   💬 **Reply**   ⬦ **Copy link**

Read 73 replies

Paul Graham (Founder of Y Combinator) is someone who I agree with on a lot of things. I also aspire someday to his level of writing skill. His perspective on venture debt is certainly valid even if I disagree with the broad generalization. In an attempt at intellectual honesty, this final chapter is focused on where a venture-lending relationship has the (rare) potential to go sideways.

PICKING THE WRONG LENDING PARTNER

Just like taking investment capital from the wrong VC fund can have very real negative impacts on a business, venture lenders are no different. There is a spectrum of players in the industry; some are amazing partners in almost any situation, a few are looking for an opportunity to take action with portfolio companies to increase their economics or perhaps even control, but most sit somewhere in the middle. I'm not going to name any particular players in this book, but if I had to guess, Paul Graham and the handful of others who are vocally against venture debt may have had run-ins with some of the bottom-tier lenders in the industry. If companies perform well or continue getting equity support, that is a non-issue, but if you hit a bump in the road, how your lender reacts becomes mission critical. I've already covered how to think about reference checks of potential partners, but I'll reiterate here that understanding who you are working with, how they act in good or bad times, and setting appropriate expectations from the start are hugely important. Who you choose to take capital from outweighs almost any other difference in pricing, structure, or commitment size.

NOT HAVING A CLEAR USE CASE

One thing that can lead to bad outcomes is not having a clear use case for the debt. Just extending runway and buying time without clear milestones to drive a successful equity fundraise and/or a higher valuation can often lead to uncomfortable situations between a company and their lender. Equity dollars should be used to fund runway for the truly unknown, while venture debt should be used to fund growth or critical product development that is tracking but needs more time. I've counseled founders repeatedly over the years on this and turned down a fair number of debt requests because there wasn't at least a semblance of strategy about what the extra dollars would help achieve. Not all lenders will hold that line and may still be willing to do the deal, but that has a higher probability of a lender getting uncomfortable and starting to think about using any ongoing defaults or even a MAC default to take control of the situation and protect their capital, to the potential detriment of the company, employees, and investors.

One of the benefits of not being required to draw down capital at the start of a lending relationship is that it gives the company time to make sure the milestones it had in mind when taking the debt are, in fact, achievable. Both the company and lender can track progress before deciding to draw down some or all the venture debt. This ensures that capital is being put to work to fund growth or progress that will lead to an increasingly likely next equity round. That is the best-case scenario for deploying venture debt to fund growth with less dilution (conveniently, the subtitle of this book).

While I won't quote him directly, I spoke with a former founder/CEO who I worked with in the past and who is now a GP at a new VC fund. He said the only heated debates at the board level that he has seen related to venture debt are about whether a company should draw the money or not. He recommended that founders and finance teams have an active dialogue with their board in the lead-up to a draw-down period coming to an end about whether it is the right time to use the capital. His perspective mirrors my own in that the only time a company should draw their venture debt is when things are going well, when putting that debt to work will help the company achieve a couple of important milestones. For example, you're in a scenario where maybe another quarter or two of revenue growth will get a larger investor set interested in the business. The pipeline is converting well and has plenty of coverage to achieve revenue targets over the next six months; additional runway extension is a good trade because you can avoid raising more money and impacting your cap table, making existing shareholders all the happier.

Don't have blinders on about the company's performance or the likelihood of being able to raise additional equity capital in the near term. I know asking founders to be realistic is a bit antithetical, but it can help avoid situations where a lender is already uncomfortable and then has a portfolio company ask to draw down a large sum. A lot of lenders will still honor that drawn-down request, likely after talking with board members, but there is a higher chance in that kind of scenario that a lender pulls the plug (via the contingency funding clause) and decides not to fund. Lenders want to avoid surprises, but so do you. Have an active ongoing dialogue with your lender about their comfort levels with the business and your future expectations about drawing down the debt.

OVER-LEVERAGING THE BUSINESS

A company can get over-leveraged in a variety of ways, but the impact is generally the same; new investors for a needed equity round balk at funding a business where a large amount of their equity dollars will go to repay debt and not to the business itself. That is a very bad place to be and will certainly lead to heated discussions between a company, their board, and their lender—the outcome of which can lead to company shutdown or sale.

How does a company get over-leveraged? Most frequently it comes from taking on too much debt from the start. Lenders may be clamoring over themselves to throw money at you, and that can be very flattering. It is hard not to get swept up in the abundance of capital being offered, even if there isn't a rational place to put it all to work; it's very similar to frothy equity markets where round sizes and valuations can increase by the day. With the increased amount of dollars offered, there is less room for error for the company to avoid over-leveraging. You are priced to perfection, as they say.

Other ways that a business can find itself with too much debt even if it was appropriately sized in the beginning include a planned revenue ramp that doesn't materialize or revenue is not as recurring or repeatable as expected. Sometimes seasonal business models, like consumer hardware or consumer goods, don't come out of the low point in the year or season as expected. Or a big macro environment shift negatively affects a particular industry and every player in it is forced to make significant changes (the effect of AI on non-AI businesses, for example). These and other factors can create a situation where a company becomes over-leveraged.

How would I define over-leveraged? We've discussed that most lenders try to keep total funded debt at or below 1:1 relative to revenue or ARR. That's a decent metric for sure. Another one that gets more directly to the crux of the issue is when debt service—that is the monthly interest payment, or if amortization has kicked in, the principal and interest payments—is greater than 35% of total operating expenses. I don't have a scientific explanation for why 35% seems to be the threshold for leverage becoming overly burdensome, but it is based on twenty-plus years in venture lending across four venture banks; this number consistently came up when companies were going sideways, a good chunk of which ultimately failed. It seems that debt service being greater than one-third of a company's operating expenses may be the psychological tipping point for investors on how much equity they are willing to tolerate being used to repay debt. Pay attention to how much of your operating expense is going toward servicing debt now and what it is projected to be in the future, in both good and bad scenarios. Avoid getting to that 35% level if possible.

IS IT REALLY WORTH IT?

At the end of the day, venture debt is just a financing tool for a company. When used correctly, it can potentially lead to great outcomes; when used poorly, it can potentially topple a business. Founders, CFOs, finance teams, and boards need to weigh when it is appropriate to take this tool out of the box and when to leave it for another day, like many of the choices start-up companies face throughout their lifetime. There is no black-and-white answer as to whether a start-up should use venture debt, only varying shades of gray. It is a judgment call that likely involves at least some risk, was a sentiment shared by Emmett Shear (then CEO at Twitch and YC portfolio company) in a reply to Paul Graham's tweet:

Paul Graham ✔ · Feb 7, 2020   X
@paulg · Follow
Venture debt is like a delicious sandwich that only costs ten cents, but occasionally explodes in your face.

If I were running a startup, I don't think I'd ever take it.

Emmett Shear ✔
@eshear · Follow

If you can avoid it, sure. Justin.tv took significant venture debt from SVB during our A' round, and I'm pretty sure we would have run out of money without it (bandwidth costs were crazy). Definitely risky, but sometimes risk is worth taking.

6:20 AM · Feb 7, 2020   ⓘ

♥ 58   💬 Reply   🔗 Copy link

Read 3 replies

AUTHOR'S NOTE

I hope you've found this book useful, mildly funny, or both. Thanks for buying a copy and taking the time to read it.

Thanks to all the entrepreneurs, CFOs, and investors who I've had the good fortune to work with over my career. Seeing you toil day and night for years to bring something new into the world continues to be inspiring. That experience helped shape what became this book.

As a first-time author, there is nothing more I appreciate than candid feedback. I'd love to know what you liked or found particularly insightful. Tell me where I made you laugh, if at all. You've also earned the right to to tell me what I got wrong, to let me know what could have used a better explanation, or to point out one of the many typos I will have certainly missed. Let me know topics you'd want to see added into a potential second edition. I will gladly consider all of it at feedback@venturedebtdeals.com.

For more resources and updates, visit venturedebtdeals.com, or learn about my advisory and speaking work at marshallhawks.com.

Finally, if you found the book to be helpful, consider leaving an Amazon or Goodreads review or simply tell a friend or colleague about it.

Onward.

ACKNOWLEDGMENTS

I bought the URL for the book title in 2018 hoping that would spark some motivation but nothing happened. I actually started writing a few chapters of this book in 2012, then . . . nothing happened. Writing, as it turns out, is *hard*. What finally got me off the fence? Venture capitalist David Hornik's great un-conference, "The Lobby," and a small group discussion there led by Sarah Lacy on how to write and publish your first book. Sarah is a successful entrepreneur, author, and now bookstore owner. After hearing her speak about writing, it is hard not to get inspired.

On the heels of The Lobby, I had a chance meeting with Matt Blumberg, a repeat entrepreneur and impressive author who also happened to be the CEO voice in *Venture Deals*. He was exceptionally kind in sharing advice and his network with me. That sequence of fortuitous conversations was the spark that led me to leave a good-paying job at a great firm to finally write a book, much to my wife's "delight."

In addition to David, Sarah, and Matt, I owe a lot to Brad Feld, venture capitalist and co-author of *Venture Deals*, who took the time to provide early advice and commentary on drafts of the book. Because *Venture Deals* was the inspiration for this book, his help in bringing it to life was humbling and invaluable.

The case studies throughout the book were brought to life from my own hazy memory and the help of a handful of people involved in them—Matt Wright, Michelle Sabourin, Andrew Curtis, Stan Kong, and Stewart Alsop.

I was fortunate to read *Write Useful Books* by Rob Fitzpatrick and Adam Rosen early on. I took their advice to use beta reading to help shape early drafts. Thanks to my beta readers: Paul Hernandez, Janet Wan, Erica Plybeah, Cathy Hawley, Rob Freelen, Rudy Haddad, John Roehm, Patrick Haggerty, Chris Canazzaro, Filip Stoj, Jacqueline Tiffin, Gabi Mandowsky, Chris Swanson, Karim Mashnuk, Ania Bytow, Jason Pan, Jose Esquer-Romero, and Mark Kiyonaga, who generously plodded through my early writing without complaint. I owe you a debt of gratitude.

Sam Angus and Eric Shedlosky at Fenwick & West and Laurie Hutchins at DLA Piper were generous with their time and contributions to the legal detail of the book. They also didn't hold it against me when I made jokes about their chosen profession, and for that I thank them.

To my writing partner and coach, Pete Birkeland: You were instrumental early on in making me believe this was possible. Your feedback and encouragement as time went on meant a lot.

My experience in venture lending in a variety of roles and institutions over more than twenty years allowed me to learn from some exceptionally smart and kind people. Mentors like Peter Kidder, Harvey Lum, Albert Martinez, Jennifer Schellenberg, and Dave Jones. Watching peers like Matt Trotter, Jackie Spencer, Jason Mok, Denny Boyle, Joe Werner, Justin Pirzadeh, Jamie Riggs, Namita Anand and Kevin Longo do amazing work helped motivate me to do better throughout my career. Their collective fingerprints are all over the experiences that helped shape this book.

I was fortunate to grow up with parents, a CEO turned venture capitalist and a former librarian, who fostered intellectual curiosity from the start. My father, in particular, gave me a front row seat to the life of an entrepreneur and investor from as early as I can remember. As a relatively new parent myself, I hope to have a similarly meaningful impact on my children.

Speaking of whom, Cooper and Iva: You are the gift that keeps on giving. To spend the past year with both of you when I wasn't writing has been a delight. For those of you on the fence about wanting a family, know that they make life better in so many ways, it's hard to fathom. Just do it.

Finally, to my wife, Michelle: Thanks for being a great mom and partner, for pushing me to stay fit when writing this book, and for your willingness to check my ego on how important my day job is compared to family. I love you and the family we've built together.

APPENDIX 1

EXAMPLE TERM SHEET—EARLY-STAGE

Borrower(s)	Company XYZ, Inc. plus any material subsidiaries
Commitment Amount	$5,000,000
Lender(s)	ABC Bank
Availability	Commitment Amount fully available at close for duration of the Draw Period. Minimum advance amount of $500,000 per advance.
Draw Period	Earlier of 18 months from close or 3-31-27.
Interest-Only Period	Earlier of 18 months from close or 3-31-27.
Borrowing Formula	None.
Repayment	At the end of the Interest-Only Period, any outstanding balance will begin amortizing across 36 equal monthly payments of principal and interest. Maturity date of the facility will be the earlier of 54 months from close or 3-31-XX.
Interest Rate	WSJ Prime + 1.00%, floating. WSJ Prime is currently 7.50% with an indicative rate of 8.50%.
Commitment Fee	$25,000 due at close of documentation.
Final Payment Fee	2% of the advanced amount due at the earlier of prepayment or full maturity.
Prepayment Fee	3% if outstanding loan balance is prepaid within 12 months of close; 2% if prepaid between 12 and 24 months from close; 1% thereafter.

Warrant	25bps of fully diluted ownership in Borrower's Common Stock.
	50% will vest at close of documentation and 50% will vest prorated based on advances.
	Strike price to be set at current 409a valuation price of $0.50 per share. Warrant will have a fixed exercise price, 10-year term and allow for cashless exercise.
Right to Invest	None.
Financial Covenants	None.
Collateral	First-priority lien on all assets with a negative pledge on intellectual property.
Events of Default	Customary affirmative and negative covenants for transactions of this nature including a Material Adverse Change Clause.
Banking Requirement	Borrower to maintain its primary operating banking relationship with the ABC Bank, including credit cards and a minimum of 80% of investable balances. Other banking relationships with greater than $250K will require Deposit Account Control Agreements.
Reporting Requirements	• Monthly financials and Compliance Certificate within 30 days of month end • Annual company prepared financials within 30 days of year end • Audited Annual Financials within 180 days of year end • Annual projections within 30 days of Board receipt/approval • Other items that Lender reasonably requests due within 30 days

Good Faith Deposit	$25,000 due at the execution of the Term Sheet to be applied toward the Expenses and Commitment Fee at close. If Lender decides not to move forward, the Good Faith Deposit will be refunded to the Company; otherwise, the Good Faith Deposit is nonrefundable.
Expenses	Borrower will pay all customary and reasonable legal, audit fees, and expenses.
Marketing	Borrower grants Lender the right to use the Borrower's logo in marketing materials and issue a tombstone and press release upon close of documentation.
Subject to	• Final diligence including investor calls • Internal ABC Bank credit approval • Satisfactory legal documentation

APPENDIX 2

EXAMPLE TERM SHEET—LATER-STAGE

Borrower(s)	Company XYZ, Inc, plus all material existing and future subsidiaries. ("Company XYZ," "Company," or "Borrower")
Commitment Amount	$75,000,000 available at close Or Tranche 1: $50,000,000 fully funded at close Tranche 2: $25,000,000 available upon Borrower hitting Performance Milestone
Use of Proceeds	General corporate purposes and Permitted Acquisitions. Definition of Permitted Acquisitions to be mutually agreed upon in definitive legal documents.
Lender(s)	Private Credit ABC Fund, and any affiliate or transferee ("Private Credit," "ABC Fund," or "Lender")
Maturity Date	48 months from close.
Interest-Only Period	Through Maturity.
Amortization Period	None. Outstanding principal balance due at Maturity or early payoff.
Interest Rate	WSJ Prime + 4.00%, floating. Indicative rate of 11.50% which will also serve as the Interest Rate Floor. Or One-month Term SOFR + 8%, floating. 2.0% can be PIK at Borrower's option. Indicative rate of 12.32%. Interest Floor of 11.50%.
Commitment Fee	1.5% of Commitment Amount paid at close.

End of Term Fee	3% of funded amount.
Prepayment Fee Or Make-Whole Provision	2% of the outstanding principal in the first 18 months of the loan; 1% of the outstanding principal after 18 months but before 36 months of close; no Prepayment Fee after 36 months from close. Or Within 12 months from close, Borrower may prepay the outstanding principal plus the current and all future interest payments. 103% of outstanding principal after 12 months until 24 months. No Prepayment Fee thereafter.
Warrant	Lender to receive warrants equal to 50bps of fully diluted ownership, granted at close in Borrower's Common Stock. Strike price to be set at current 409a valuation price of $0.01 per share, have a 10-year term, allow for cashless exercise with automatic termination at IPO or sale.
Right to Invest	Borrower shall grant Lender the right, but not the obligation, to invest up to $2,000,000 in the next round of equity financing on the same terms offered to other Preferred investors. Or 5% of the Commitment Amount in future equity rounds.

Borrowing Formula	None Or Borrower's Debt Outstanding shall not exceed 90% of ARR (ARR defined as trailing 3 months revenue multiplied by four) for first 12 months from close and then shall not exceed 80% of ARR after 12 months from close. If, at any time, Borrower's Debt Outstanding exceeds the ARR thresholds, Borrower shall immediately repay Debt Outstanding until it is equal to or less than the respective threshold level.
Financial Covenants	None Or Customary affirmative and negative covenants for transaction of this type, including: · Minimum Unrestricted Cash = $15,000,000 · Revenue Coverage (Trailing 3-month annualized GAAP revenue) / Outstanding Debt > 2.5× for first 12 months and > 3× thereafter Or None. Cross-defaulted with Senior Lender covenants.

Collateral	Perfected first-priority lien on all assets, including intellectual property. Or Perfected second-priority lien on all of Borrower's assets, including intellectual property. Lender's security interest shall sit behind a first lien credit facility not to exceed XXX.
Reporting Requirements	• Audited Financials within 180 days • Quarterly unaudited financials within 30 days • Monthly financials within 30 days • 409a valuation report within 30 days of issuance • Board decks within 30 days of Board meeting • Cap table within 30 days of new issuance and within 30 days of every fiscal year end • Other financial information reasonably requested by Lender
Expenses	Borrower will pay all customers and reasonable legal, audit fees, UCC search costs, filing costs, and miscellaneous expenses.
Due Diligence Fee	$75,000 due at execution of term sheet. The Due Diligence Fee will be applied toward the Commitment Fee and is nonrefundable except in the case where Lender does not approve the proposed transaction.
Closing Time Frame	Loan closing date will be later than 30 days from execution of this term sheet unless extended by Lender.
Marketing	Borrower grants Lender the right to use the Borrower's logo in marketing materials and issue a tombstone and press release upon close of documentation.

Legal	Customary affirmative and negative covenants for transactions of this nature, including a Material Adverse Change Clause and restrictions on certain business activities including without limitation, restrictions on liens and indebtedness, payment of cash dividends, asset dispositions and down streaming, guaranties, mergers etc.
Exclusivity	Borrower also agrees that until the 30th day from the execution of this term sheet (unless extended in conjunction with the Loan Closing Date extension that has been mutually agreed to by Lender and Borrower), (the "Exclusivity Period") it will not (a) solicit or entertain any proposal, (b) negotiate with any other person, or (c) provide any information with respect to Borrower to any person who might be expected to propose alternate financing, or Borrower shall pay Lender an amount equal to the Commitment Fee and the Due Diligence Fee.
Subject to	• Satisfactory diligence to include investor calls • Formal investment committee approval • Satisfactory legal documentation

APPENDIX 3

MARSHALL'S PORTFOLIO COMPANIES OVER THE YEARS

This non-exhaustive list includes a collection of companies I was fortunate enough to work with over the past twenty-plus years. I was the lead banker on those lending relationships and all used venture debt during their life cycle. I've included this to give you a sense of the relative prevalence of venture debt, as well as the number of data points that inform the perspective you find throughout this book. Inclusion of a company in this list does not imply its endorsement of this book or its contents. Also, please forgive the humble brag.

- Adara Media (ACQ:RateGain)
- Airbnb (IPO:ABNB)
- Airware (ACQ:Delair)
- Apartment List
- Aryaka Networks
- August Lock (ACQ:Assa Abloy)
- Cantaloupe (ACQ:SB Software)
- Chariot (ACQ:Ford)
- Clearco
- Cloudflare (IPO:NET)
- Crunchbase
- Datameer
- DataStax (ACQ:IBM)
- Egnyte
- EzHome
- Fitbit (IPO:FIT->ACQ:Google)
- Fleetsmith (ACQ:Apple)
- Flurry Analytics (ACQ:Yahoo)
- GigaOm
- GreyStripe (ACQ:ValueClick)
- HighFive
- Hired
- Hover
- HyTrust (ACQ:Entrust)

- InfluxData
- Inkling
- Innovium (ACQ:Marvell)
- Kno (ACQ: Intel)
- Koho Financial
- Kontagent (ACQ:Upsight)
- LIftopia
- Fig (ACQ:Republic)
- Lucidworks
- Mavrx
- Nerdwallet (IPO:NRDS)
- NitroPDF (IPO:NTO)
- Okta (IPO:OKTA)
- OneWheel
- Oodle
- OOMA (IPO:OOMA)
- OpenDNS (ACQ:Cisco)
- Osmo (ACQ:Byju)
- People.ai
- Pi Charging
- Planet Labs (IPO:PL)
- Platfora (ACQ:Workday)
- Presence Learning
- PropertyBridge (ACQ: MoneyGram)
- Punchh (ACQ:PAR Technology)
- RetailNext
- RocketLawyer
- ServiceMax (ACQ:GE)
- Shape Security (ACQ:F5 Networks)
- ShareThis
- Simplrr
- SmartBiz (fka Billfloat)
- Spire Global (IPO:SPIR)
- Threatmetrix (ACQ:LexisNexis)
- Thumbtack
- Tote Technologies
- TubeMogul (IPO:TUBE->ACQ:Adobe)
- Twitch (ACQ:Amazon)
- VentureBeat
- VSCO
- World Golf Tour (ACQ:TopGolf)

NOTES ON SOURCES

The case studies and examples in this book draw from memory and publicly available information from a variety of sources. I've relied on databases such as Crunchbase, PitchBook, CB Insights, and Capital IQ, as well as press releases, SEC filings, news coverage, and company websites. Fundraising dates, round sizes, and valuations are taken from the best publicly reported information at the time of writing. While details may differ slightly across databases, I've chosen figures that are consistent with the most widely cited sources. All opinions, interpretations, and commentary are my own.

INDEX

A

ABF (asset-based financing) 178–180
Affirm 184
AI (artificial intelligence) 191, 204, 213
Airbnb 61–71. *See also* case studies
amortization 14, 84, 213
Arcadia 178
ARR (annual recurring revenue) 14, 57, 82, 201, 213
attornies. *See* legal counsel

B

bankruptcy-remote SPV 179
banks. *See* lenders
boards of directors
  lenders and 33, 37, 49, 54, 121
  MAC clauses 136
  nonexistent 199–200
  "orphaned" companies and 197–199
  support of, alignment with 129, 137, 157, 161, 164, 185, 194
bonds 106
borrowers 75–76
borrowing formulas
  commitment amounts 77, 82
  financial covenants 87
  lines of credit 8, 179

performance indicators, milestones 79
bridge financing 24, 114, 117, 185
Business Development Bank of Canada 11
business development departments 41–43
business models
  companies' 19, 56, 213
  lenders' 10–13, 177–179, 190

C

Cadieux, Marc 116
Canada 11, 108, 181, 187, 192
capital. *See also* fundraising, financing
  cap tables 31, 53–54, 145, 199
  cost of 10
  tranches 77
  venture capital 7, 13, 111, 191
case studies
  Airbnb 61–71
  Clearco 177–178, 180–192
  collaborating 28, 191–192
  committee members at meetings 70
  communication 156–157, 191–192
  diversifying banking 118
  educating, understanding lenders 28, 69, 70
  entrepreneurship is hard 157

fundraising too much too
quickly 191
keeping promises 27
Marshall's mistake 25
network effects 27
over-leveraging 190–191
"Phone Tap" 152–157
Silicon Valley Bank 105–118
Twitch 18–28
venture debt + equity 27
venture debt market 116
certificates 160–162, 161, 164
checks and balances 44
Chesky, Brian 62
The China Business Conundrum
(Wilcox) 115
clauses. *See also* legal counsel
confidentiality 32, 150
contingency funding 137–139,
149
exclusivity, no-shop 150–151
investor abandonment 135–137
material adverse change (MAC)
130–133
Clearco 177–178, 180–192
closing conditions 149
closing time frame 147
collateral 139–143, 160–162, 164
Comdisco 2
commercial banks. *See* lenders
commitment amount, availability
77–80, 82, 91
commitment fees 91
communication 47, 156,
164, 167–171, 191. *See
also* relationships
companies/entrepreneurs
boards of directors
lenders and 33, 37, 49, 54, 121
MAC clauses 136
nonexistent 199–200
"orphaned" companies and

197–199
support of, alignment with
129, 137, 157, 161, 164,
185, 194
business models 19, 56, 213
comps, competition 58–59, 86,
174
corporate structure chart 33
credit card programs 126
customers 33, 37
debt vs. revenue 200–201
defaulting, troubled 47, 128–
130, 132–133, 135–137,
139–141, 153
earlier-, later-stage defined 51
e-commerce businesses 180
entrepreneurship is hard 157,
167
innovation economy, market 1,
19, 27, 61, 107–108, 204
in-person meetings 45, 65
lender ownership stakes 24, 37,
97, 99–100, 196
logos, marketing 148
Marshall's clients 231–232
mid-stage 51, 195
"orphaned" companies 197–199
over-leveraging 190–191,
212–213
performance indicators,
milestones
commitment amount 77, 79
draw downs 84, 211
financial covenants 86–87,
146
KPIs 56–57
performance to plan 57, 122,
139, 172
proactive 168–169
promising vs. delivering
171–172
runway of 7, 9, 84, 87, 135, 194

security deposits 64
start-ups
  audits 121
  difficulties of 8, 49, 128, 157, 167
  entity chart 76
  later-stage 12
  red flags 58, 59, 194–201
  tech economy 2
contract terms 127–130
convertible notes 140, 161
covenants, financial 85–88, 146
Credigy 180
credit
  corporate credit card programs 126
  credit agreements 131, 145, 159, 161
  credit officers (COs) 38, 41, 44–47
  credit ratings, external 179
  creditworthiness 7, 10, 44–47, 66, 180
  letters of credit 64
  lines of credit 8, 154, 179
Cruise Automation 27
Curtis, Andrew 185, 186, 191
customers 33, 37

D

DACAs (deposit account control agreements) 124, 161
default 127–130, 132–133, 135–137, 139–141, 153
Delima, Tanay 177
deposits 102–103, 118, 124, 161
diligence
  customer, investor reference calls 33, 37, 54–56
  diligence list 31–34
  due diligence fees 102–103
  evaluating founders, business 59, 63
  internal approval, final 37–38
  investigating lenders 49, 87
  meetings and committee members 70
  screenings, initial 30–31, 43
dilution 9, 27, 96–97, 99, 177, 211
DLA Piper LLP (US) 5, 119, 130, 162
Dragon's Den (TV show) 181
draw downs. *See* venture debt
D'Souza, Andrew 177, 182

E

early termination fees 93
e-commerce businesses 180
Emergence Capital 178
equity. *See* fundraising, financing
expiry dates 147–148
Export Development Canada 11

F

facility fees 91
FDIC (Federal Deposit Insurance Corporation) 113, 115, 117, 126
Federal Reserve 106
fees 91–96, 102
Feld, Brad 1
Feng, Charlie 177
Fenwick & West 5, 119, 162
financial covenants 85–88, 139, 146. *See also* performance indicators, measurements
financial crisis (2008) 107, 173
financial statements 31, 33, 52, 56–57, 120, 183
fintech 177, 191
First Citizens Bank 21, 116
founders. *See* companies/ entrepreneurs
409a valuations 31, 54, 99, 122

fundraising, financing
  ABF (asset-based financing)
    178–180
  bridge financing 24, 114, 117,
    185
  government-backed funds 11
  lenders vet pipeline? 173
  letters of credit ("LC") 64
  "non-dilutive" 9, 27, 96, 99, 177,
    211
  "seed" rounds 12, 51, 199
  Series A, B ... 11, 51, 155, 178,
    180, 181, 199
  timelines 38–40, 147, 149, 163
  too much too quickly 191, 212
  venture debt vs. 9, 13, 27, 29

G

Gebbia, Joe 65, 70
Gerth, Bill 63, 65, 70
good faith deposits (GFDs)
  102–103
Google 24–25
government-backed funds 11
Graham, Paul 209–210, 214
Gritsiniak, Ivan 177

H

Highland Capital 178
historical financials 31, 57. *See
  also* financial statements
HSBC 115, 117
Hutchins, Laurie 119, 162

I

incorporation, articles of 31, 54
indication of interest (IOI) 34–35
indicative terms 34
innovation economy, market 1,
  19, 27, 61, 107–108, 204
Inovia 186

intellectual property (IP) 139
inter-creditor agreement 144
interest-only (IO) periods 14–15,
  82–83
interest rates 89–91, 106, 114
investors/investments. *See
  also* boards of directors; *See
  also* lenders
  investment committee (IC) 38, 41
  investment pitch deck 31
  investor abandonment clause
    135–137
  limited partners 11, 44, 80, 90
  MAC clause debate 136
  off-balance sheet options 126
  right to buy, invest 68, 96, 101
  single main, lead investor
    195–197
  third-party investors 11, 68
  vintage year funds 53
iPhones 20

J

Jobs, Steve 20
junior lenders 139, 143–146
Justin.tv 18–19, 22–23, 214

K

Kan, Justin 18
Kidder, Peter 65, 70
Kong, Stan 65, 70
KPIs (key performance indicators)
  56–57
Kurzweil, Ethan 23

L

landlord waivers 161
Leerink, Jeff 116
Leerink Partners 116
legal counsel
  best practices 162–165

clauses 131–132, 135–137, 138–139
collateral 141–142, 160–162
cost of 39–40
drafting documents 36, 38
event of default 129–130
lien on IP 141–142
lenders. *See also* venture debt; *See also* Silicon Valley Bank (SVB)
alternative 177–179, 190
announcing deals 148
approval authority 41, 46, 79
banks
    banking requirements 123–126
    deposits, deposit agreements 10, 118, 124, 161
    off-balance sheet investment options 126
    relationships with 68
boards of directors 33, 37, 49, 54, 121
business model types 10–13, 177–179, 190
choosing, vetting 49, 191, 203–208, 210
communication, relationship with 47, 156–157, 164, 167–171, 174–175, 191
creditworthiness determinations 7, 51–60, 59, 63
disbelief, suspending 28, 62
educating, understanding 28, 69, 70
fees, interest rates 89–96, 103–104
financial crisis (2008) 107, 173
funding amounts, requirements 14, 80
government-backed funds 11
in-person meetings 65–66

"lenders of last resort" 100
lien holder positions, seniority 139, 143–146, 156, 206–208
limited partners 11, 44, 80, 91
list of 16–17
Marshall's roles at SVB 19, 110, 153
meeting with quarterly 169
motivations of 70
ownership stakes 24, 37, 97, 99–100, 196
private credit funds
    defined 11–13
    later-stage start-ups 12
    third-party, LP investors 11, 68, 90
red-flagged by 58, 59, 194–201
referrals from 173
reputation 27, 30, 34, 75, 149, 205
revenue-based finance products 177
right to buy, invest 68, 96–102
securitization market 179
troubled, defaulting companies 47, 128–130, 139–141, 153
underwriters 12, 38, 43–44, 60, 88
visiting businesses 59, 62
Yosemite Sam 171
Lending Club 184
letter of credit ("LC") 64
lien holders, first/second priority 139, 143–146, 156, 206–208
limited partners 11, 44, 80, 91
lines of credit 8, 154, 179
Lin, Kevin 26
liquidity thresholds 86
live streaming platforms 18
loan origination departments 41–43
Looney Tunes 171

M

MAC (materially adverse change) clauses 130–133
"make whole provision" 93
marketing 148–149
Martin, Bill 106
maturity dates 85
Mayer, Marissa 25
MCAs (merchant cash advances) 178, 181
Mendelson, Jason 1
Microsoft 23
milestones. *See* performance indicators, measurements
MUFG 117
Musk, Elon 167

N

National Bank 117
NDAs (non-disclosure agreements) 32
negotiations 147, 162, 164, 205–206
Nijjar, Karam 186
notes, convertible 140, 161

O

Oak HC/FT 180
originators, loan 42–44
OSFI (Office of the Superintendent of Financial Institutions) 115, 187
over-leveraging 190–191, 212–213
ownership stakes 24, 37, 97, 99–100, 196

P

Paik, Chris 23
payment in kind (PIK) 91
penny strike warrants 101
performance indicators, measurements
commitment amount 77, 79
draw downs 84, 211
financial covenants 86–87, 146
KPIs 56–57
performance to plan 57, 122, 139, 172
personal guarantee requests 203
"Phone Tap" 152–157
Pinegrove Capital Partners 71, 116
PlayStation 23
portfolio management 43–44, 47
prepayment fees 92–94
primary source of repayment (PSOR) 52
projections 31, 87, 138. *See also* performance indicators, measurements
put options 100–101

Q

Qatalyst Partners 24
Quattrone, Frank 24

R

Raging Capital Ventures 106
RBCx 117
reference checks 49, 87, 144. *See also* diligence
relationships
banking, DACAs 124, 161
with lenders 47, 68, 156, 164, 167–171, 191–192
maintaining 22, 27
Marshall and SVB 19, 110, 152
"orphaned" companies 197–199
RMs, portfolio managers 43–44, 47
repayments
"bullet repayment" structure 84
early termination, prepayment

fees 92–94
length of 84–85
sources of 52–53, 194, 200
reporting requirements 120–123, 128
reputation 27, 30, 34, 75, 149, 205
right to buy, invest 68, 96–102
risk management
  bank diversification 118
  draw downs, interest-only periods 81, 83
  events of default 127
  innovation companies 97
  "lenders of last resort" 100
  over-leveraging 190–191, 212–213
  ownership stakes 24, 37, 97, 99–100, 196
  reputational risk 27, 30, 34, 75, 149, 205
  risk indicators 171, 194–201
  risk profile, rating 46, 84, 122
  risk tolerance 60, 87, 128, 130, 169
RML (remaining months liquidity) test 87
Romanow, Michele 177, 181, 182, 186

S

screenings, initial 30–31, 43
secondary source of repayment (SSOR) 52
securitization market 179
security agreements 161
"seed" rounds 12, 51, 199
Seibel, Michael 18, 27
Sequoia Capital 62
Shanghai Pudong Development Bank (SPDB) 115
shareholders 31, 53, 54, 196–197, 200. See also stocks

Shear, Emmett 18, 23, 26, 27, 214
Shedlosky, Eric 119, 162
Siebel, Michael 21–22
Sigfstead, Curt 182
Silicon Valley Bank (SVB)
  case study 105–118
  employees 108, 111, 115, 116
  error of 114
  First Citizens 21
  foreign offices 108
  founded 1
  lending stance 21, 62, 67
  Marshall's roles 19, 110, 153
  stock drops, billions $ lost 111
  SVB Canada 110–112, 117, 181, 187
  SVB Capital 71, 187
  SVBFG 187
  SVB Financial Group 115
  SVB Ski House 175
Socialcam 20–22, 23
Social Capital 178
Softbank 181
Sony 23
"special" groups 47–49
SPVs (special purpose vehicles) 179
start-ups. See companies/entrepreneurs
Stifel 117
stocks
  common 101, 140
  preferred 122, 140, 156, 161
subjective default 130, 132–133, 135–137
subject to's 149
subordination agreement 161

T

term sheets. See also legal counsel
  amortization period 84–85
  banking requirements 123–125
  borrower(s) section 75–76

borrowing formulas
  commitment amounts 77, 82
  financial covenants 87
  lines of credit 8, 179
  performance indicators, mile-
    stones 79
closing conditions, time frame
  147, 149
collateral 139–143, 160–162, 164
commitment amount, availability 77–78, 79–80, 82, 91
confidentiality clause 150
draw downs
  contingency funding clauses
    137–139, 149
  defined 14
  drawdown debates 211
  interest-only period 14, 83
  length of 14–15, 80–82
  options, requirements 80, 211
  vesting warrants 98
events of default 127–130
examples of 221–223, 225–229
exclusivity, no-shop clauses
  150–151
expiry dates 147–148
fees 91–96, 102
financial covenants 76, 85–88
good faith deposits (GFDs)
  102–103
indication of interest (IOI) vs.
  35
interest period, rates 82–83,
  89–91
investor abandonment clause
  135–137
lender's section, expenses
  78–79, 103–104
MAC (materially adverse
  change) clauses 130–133
marketing 148–149
maturity date 85

negotiations 147, 162, 164,
  205–206
nonbinding 74, 75
personal guarantee requests 203
preamble 74–75
reporting requirements 120–
  123, 128
required funds at close 80
right to buy, invest 68, 96–102
use of proceeds 78
warrants 96–102, 161, 165
tertiary source of repayment
  (TSOR) 52
Thrive Capital 23
trailing 12-month revenue 14, 77,
  84, 201
tranches 77
Trotter, Matt 61
Twitch 18–28, 214. See also case
  studies
Twitter 105

U

uncommitted accordion 77–78
underwriters 12, 38, 43–44, 60, 88
unrealized losses 106
up-front fees 91–92, 102
Upper90 178

V

Venture Deals (Feld & Mendelson)
  1
venture capital 7, 13, 111, 191. See
  also fundraising, financing
venture debt. See also lenders
  best practices 162–165
  choosing lender 49, 191–192,
    203, 210
  clear use case 210–212
  corporate decision buyoffs 21
  current market 117
  customer acquisition tool 11

definition of 1–2, 7–8
downsides of 209–214
draw downs
  contingency funding clause 149
  defined 14
  drawdown debates 211
  interest-only period 14, 83
  length of 14–15, 80–82
  options, requirements 80, 211
  vesting warrants 98
fundraise vs. 9, 13, 27, 29
government-backed funds 11
legal processes 159–165
lender list 16–17
mechanics of 13–15, 29–39
negotiations 164
"non-dilutive financing" 9, 27,
    96–101, 99, 177, 211
over-leveraging 190–191,
    212–213
timelines 38–40, 147, 149, 163
video games 18, 23
vintage year funds 53
Vogt, Kyle 18, 27

W

waivers, landlord 161
warrants 96–102, 161, 165
Western Technology Investment
    (WTI) 1
WhatsApp 111
Wilcox, Ken 115
workout groups 49

X

Xbox 23

Y

Yahoo 25
Y-Combinator 21, 27, 61, 210

ABOUT THE AUTHOR

Marshall Hawks has spent over twenty years in venture banking and lending. The bulk of that time was at Silicon Valley Bank, where he held nine different roles in three countries over sixteen years. Most recently, he led SVB's Relationship Management organization in Northern California and oversaw the bank's in-house private credit team, the Strategic Capital Group. Before that, he spent three years building SVB's Canada Branch as Head of Credit Solutions—the best, only, and token American north of the border.

Over the course of his career, Marshall has worked and provided debt capital to hundreds of high-growth start-ups, including Airbnb, Twitch, Fitbit, Planet Labs, Tubemogul, and Egnyte. Those experiences gave him a front-row seat to how founders use—and sometimes misuse—venture debt. Those lessons helped shape this book.

Prior to joining SVB in 2009, Marshall worked in venture lending roles at Wells Fargo, Greater Bay Venture Banking (acquired by Wells), and Comerica Bank. He holds a degree in economics from Sonoma State University, which mostly means he can draw an impressive graph and knows that incentives matter.

Marshall is also the founder of Writing is Hard Publishing, the imprint he created to publish *Venture Debt Deals*. Besides writing, he occasionally speaks with founders, finance teams, and investors about the role of debt in start-up financing and the broader lessons he has drawn from two decades in innovation banking.

Outside of work, Marshall is an avid skier, soccer player, and longtime CrossFit enthusiast who enjoys lifting oddly shaped heavy objects—including his two young children. He lives in San Francisco with his wife, Michelle, and their family.

Readers interested in updates, resources, or speaking opportunities can visit venturedebtdeals.com or marshallhawks.com.